The ADHD *Companion*™

Attention Deficit Hyperactivity Disorder

Molly Lyle Brown

Content Area: ADHD

Ages: 5 through 18

Grades: K through 12

D1088792

LinguiSystems, Inc.
3100 4th Avenue
East Moline, IL 61244-9700
1-800-PRO IDEA
1-800-776-4332

FAX: 1-800-577-4555
E-mail: service@linguisystems.com
Web: www.linguisystems.com
TDD: 1-800-933-8331
(for those with hearing impairments)

Printed in the U.S.A.

ISBN 0-7606-0461-4

About the Author

Molly's version of "hands-on" teaching!

Today I am a high school resource teacher at Clinton High School in Clinton, Iowa, doing what every teacher today is doing — surviving. Budgets are tight, the workload is ever increasing, and with that our jobs are more complex and demanding than ever. Together, we special educators and regular educators must meet the needs of a variety of students in our classrooms. That takes time, energy, and commitment which every one of you gives without question as a teacher today. It is my hope that this book will help your teaching life be a bit easier, allow you to enjoy your students, and leave you with time to enjoy your family, friends, and life in general.

My almost 28 years in the education field has included teaching high school English and working as a resource teacher with students with special needs like learning disabilities, attention deficit hyperactivity disorder (ADHD), and autism. I have also worked as a writer and editor for LinguiSystems.

I have used my educational expertise to write and publish *100 Activities for Transition* with Hawthorne Educational Services, Inc., Columbia, MO, and *The LD Teacher's IEP Companion*, *The LD Teacher's IDEA Companion — K-5*, and *The LD Teacher's IDEA Companion — 6-12* with LinguiSystems, Inc. One day I hope to be teaching at the college level and making educational presentations to show others how to make inclusion and collaboration work in the regular classroom.

When I'm not busy teaching and writing, I spend time with my three wonderful daughters and running after two granddaughters and a grandson. I also enjoy collecting dolls, flower gardening, socializing with my buddies, and running and biking.

Dedication

This book is dedicated to my brother and his wife, Dave and Anne Brown, and to their son Daniel. Dave and Annie have shown incredible devotion and love for their son who has ADHD and who has come so very far in his 16 years. I'm so glad I'm related to you, Dan!

Table of Contents

Introduction 5

Attention Deficit Hyperactivity Disorder (ADHD): Diagnosis and Treatment 5
What Students with ADHD Are Really Like 13
How to Use *The ADHD Companion* 17

Adapting the Classroom Environment
Chapter 1: Classroom Routines 19
Chapter 2: Teacher and Class Selection 34
Chapter 3: The Classroom Environment 38

Developing and Improving Skills
Chapter 4: Attention Skills 42
Chapter 5: Organizational Skills 55
Chapter 6: Social Skills 67
Chapter 7: Memory Skills 87
Chapter 8: Work Completion Skills 107

Meeting Academic Needs
Chapter 9: Mathematics 127
Chapter 10: Reading and Literature 140
Chapter 11: Science and Social Studies 157
Chapter 12: Writing 172
Chapter 13: Physical Education 188

Enlisting Parent Support
Chapter 14: Communicating with Parents 193
Chapter 15: Providing Academic Support at Home 196
Chapter 16: Fostering Appropriate Behavior at Home and at School 205

Resources 215

References 216

Introduction

Twenty or so years ago when I was first teaching high school students with learning disabilities, I had my first student with attention deficit hyperactivity disorder (ADHD). Did I know it at the time? No. I knew Dan was different. Other students didn't know what to make of him. He was bright, he was jittery, he was impulsive, he was very talkative, and he never brought tissues with him to handle the never-ending nose drip related to his allergies. He sought out the bathroom for paper towels to handle that problem, but I have a feeling he was really handling his need to move in addition to taking care of his nose. At that time, we "professionals" knew less than Dan about how to handle what eventually came to be called attention deficit hyperactivity disorder.

What is ADHD, how is it diagnosed and what do we do about it? What follows is this special educator's semi-simplistic "spin" on the state of ADHD today.

Attention Deficit Hyperactivity Disorder (ADHD): Diagnosis and Treatment

What is ADHD?

Medically speaking, ADHD is a neurobiological disability that affects three to five percent of school-aged children and two to four percent of adults. In layman's terms, it is a medical condition with far-reaching effects on an individual's health, behavior, academic achievement, psychological well-being, and social acceptance. ADHD is a condition so pervasive that it affects the individual's entire daily life including home life, social life, and academic and work settings.

In general, ADHD refers to a condition in which an individual has developmentally inappropriate attention levels. It does not mean there is an overall lack of attention. It means the individual has problems with paying attention. He may pay attention too little or too much. Such an individual needs to learn how to adjust attention appropriately. Generally, he finds it hard to control focus and concentration.

ADHD is found as two basic types.

- AD/HD-I — the inattentive type
- AD/HD-HI — a more serious and complex condition because of hyperactivity and impulsivity

ADHD occurs across all levels of intelligence including the bright and gifted. Even so, these students' inattentiveness, impulsivity, and hyperactivity may cause failing grades, grade retention, and discipline problems resulting in suspension or expulsion.

What traits suggest a student may have ADHD?

A variety of traits may suggest ADHD, but a lengthy diagnostic process must be followed to make a definite diagnosis. Some traits you may observe include:

- impulsivity
- overreacting to stimuli
- rigidity or inability to make changes easily
- disorders or inconsistencies in levels of attention and concentration
- distractibility
- excessive motor activity or hyperactivity
- poor social skills
- poor planning and organizational skills
- slow speed of cognitive processing
- memory problems
- obsessive thinking in the form of persistence or perseveration
- daydreaming and excessive internal focus
- inconsistency

Teachers typically see classroom behaviors like poor listening skills, illegible handwriting, forgetfulness, daydreaming, a poor sense of time, and having trouble making transitions as indicators of possible ADHD.

How is a diagnosis of ADHD made?

The diagnosis of ADHD requires input from a team of people usually with the student's primary physician directing the process. At times, school personnel may make a referral to the student's parents who in turn involve the physician. However the process is initiated, it usually includes the gathering of information in these ways:

- a complete medical history and exam
- school data like grades and behavior
- questionnaires of teachers and parents
- psychological testing (possibly including IQ and academic testing to measure achievement in the areas of reading, math, spelling, and writing)
- other tests to check for learning disabilities

Since many things can cause a student to be inattentive, the diagnostic process helps rule out boredom, learning disabilities, or emotional difficulties as causes of ADHD.

Once information has been gathered during the diagnostic process, criteria from the *Diagnostic and Statistical Manual of the American Psychiatric Association*, 4th Edition (DSM-IV 1994) is referred to.

The following criteria are for **AD/HD: Predominantly Hyperactive-Impulsive Type (AD/HD-HI)**:

a. often fidgets with hands or feet or squirms in seat

b. often leaves seat in classroom or in other situations in which remaining seated is expected

c. often runs about or climbs excessively in situations in which it is inappropriate (in adolescents or adults, may be limited to subjective feelings of restlessness)

d. often has difficulty playing or engaging in leisure activities quietly

e. often "on the go" or often acts as if "driven by a motor"

f. often talks excessively

g. often blurts out answers before questions have been completed

h. often has difficulty awaiting turn

i. often interrupts or intrudes on others

The following criteria are for **AD/HD: Predominantly Inattentive (AD/HD-I)**:

a. often fails to give close attention to details or makes careless mistakes in schoolwork, work, or other activities

b. often has difficulty sustaining attention in tasks or play activities

c. often does not seem to listen when spoken to directly

d. often does not follow through on instructions and fails to finish schoolwork, chores, or duties in the workplace (not due to oppositional behavior or failure to understand instructions)

e. often has difficulty organizing tasks and activities

f. often avoids, dislikes, or is reluctant to engage in tasks that require sustained mental effort (e.g., schoolwork or homework)

g. often loses things necessary for tasks or activities (e.g., toys, school assignments, pencils, books, tools)

h. often distracted by extraneous stimuli

i. often forgetful in daily activities

Used widely by family doctors, pediatricians, psychologists, and psychiatrists to diagnose ADHD with or without hyperactivity, the DSM-IV further indicates that:

- symptoms must have been in existence for at least six months with onset of at least some of the symptoms occurring before age seven

- symptoms are observed in two or more settings (e.g., home and school)
- there is significant impairment in social or academic functioning
- symptoms are not caused by a pervasive development disorder (PDD) or other psychological disorder, including anxiety or depression

Are there any positives associated with ADHD?

Definitely! We need to keep the positives in mind when someone tells us a student has ADHD. I have thoroughly enjoyed most of my students with ADHD for a variety of reasons, and their positive attributes generally far outweighed the kinds of challenges they brought me. Their positive attributes may include:

- high levels of intelligence
- personable personalities
- being very articulate and verbal
- having lots of energy and enthusiasm
- expressing themselves through creativity
- spontaneity and excitement in living in the moment
- intense focus on what they're involved with

How is ADHD "treated"?

Because ADHD affects the student's entire daily life including home life, social life, and academic and work settings, it is crucial to use a multidisciplinary team approach to meet all his needs. From an educational perspective, that means school personnel, with the help of the student's parents, are responsible for meeting the student's academic, behavioral, and social needs.

Educational Alternatives for Students with ADHD

Three options are available for students with ADHD.

- placement in regular education with no accommodations
- placement in regular education with a 504 plan providing for accommodations
- special education placement with an IEP (Individual Education Plan) providing for accommodations and/or special class placement

However, if a student's attention deficit is causing significant educational and behavioral problems at school, more specialized services and accommodations via a 504 plan or IEP must be seriously considered.

504 Plans vs. Special Education

Two public laws exist that outline provisions for the "free and appropriate education for all individuals with disabilities." Both laws allow for the placement of students with ADHD in regular educational programs.

Section 504 of the Rehabilitation Act of 1973 has general guidelines which state that anyone who believes he has a handicap that interferes with "one or more major life activities" like learning, is eligible for accommodations. As a result, a 504 plan is created, usually with the involvement of the student's parents, a guidance counselor, and regular education teachers. The 504 plan describes the student's disability and needs, and lists accommodations that will be made by regular education personnel like teachers and counselors.

The Individuals with Disabilities Act (IDEA) of 1990 has stricter requirements for placing students with ADHD. These students, in addition to having ADHD, must also qualify for services as a result of learning disabilities, health impairment, or emotional impairment, and a severe discrepancy must exist between the student's ability and actual achievement.

Once a student qualifies under IDEA, an IEP is created describing the extent of special education and regular education programming, as well as accommodations regular education teachers will be expected to make. Involved in the IEP planning are a variety of people who will provide direct services to the student. IEP team members include special education teachers, regular education teachers where appropriate, the school psychologist, the social worker, the guidance counselor, the student, and her parents.

Accommodations that may be provided for the student with ADHD under either a 504 plan or an IEP may include variations in the following areas.

- methods of instruction
- methods of presentation
- behavioral management systems
- classroom rules and expectations
- types of instructional materials
- conditions and means of taking tests
- grading criteria

The biggest differences between the laws which provide services for students with ADHD are how much support can be provided and by whom.

Which educational alternative is better?

Both laws provide for accommodations within the regular classroom and both laws create more individualized plans for the student with ADHD based on the input of a multidisciplinary team.

However, as long as the student legitimately qualifies, I prefer seeing a student with ADHD placed in special education and served through an IEP. Here's why.

- The ratio of special education teacher to students is usually significantly lower than the number of students a regular education teacher must deal with every day. Consequently, the student can be monitored more closely and provided with more direct individualized services to meet his needs.

- Special education teachers are already trained to make accommodations and use strategies for students with needs like ADHD. They are more available to help the student with ADHD, as well as be a consultant to regular education teachers.

- Besides educational accommodations, some students with ADHD also require behavioral management plans to help them learn appropriate behaviors and extinguish those behaviors that interfere with learning and socialization. These behavioral management plans are most consistently and effectively carried out through a team of special educators, regular educators, and often the school psychologist or consultant.

- IEP placement generates extra funds for serving students in special education. Individualized accommodations can include the need to purchase different materials and technology for student use. 504 Plans are not backed by special funding, so students get only "reasonable accommodations" that regular education can provide.

What else is involved in treatment for students with ADHD?

Besides the student's educational needs, his medical, psychological, behavioral, and emotional needs must be addressed. Students with ADHD often have trouble with peers, they may have self-esteem issues, they may experience conflict in the classroom, and they may need medication to help them more appropriately focus their attention and concentration. Consequently, having parents highly involved is crucial. It is because of this crucial need for parents to foster the student's overall success and to follow through on the student's "treatment" at home that the Enlisting Parent Support section of this book, pages 193-214, has been provided.

The use of medication with a student with ADHD and the provision of counseling for a student having emotional, peer, or self-esteem problems are both highly emotionally-charged issues for parents. They also are areas where we educators and support personnel can only make recommendations and not the ultimate decisions, despite what we perceive is in a student's best interests.

Parents often have mixed feelings about having their child take medication. Many parents don't like the idea of their child taking any kind of medication. They may dislike perceived harmful physical effects of medication, though most medications used today have minimal serious side effects. They may feel that as long as the school does what's "right" for their child, he won't need it, or they may have the belief that he'll "grow out of" his behavioral or attention difficulties. They may not realize how significant or pervasive the child's attention problem is within the school setting (that's where our communication comes in). Having to take medication may make the child feel too different, and parents often sympathize with their child's need for peer acceptance.

Some parents may feel the stigma, too, of having not only a child that needs special education accommodations, but also one that requires medication. Furthermore, some students need counseling that may involve the rest of the family at times. The total treatment of a student with ADHD can be overwhelming for a family and the child. As a result, our role is to be as supportive as we can be within the limits the family allows and with as much support of the student's educational needs as possible.

Discipline Issues

Discipline and behavioral issues will arise inevitably with some students with ADHD, particularly those with high levels of impulsivity and hyperactivity. Two things should be kept in mind when dealing with behavior and discipline.

Incompetence vs. Noncompliance   There is a significant difference between a student being incompetent or unskilled in appropriate behavior and a student who knowingly chooses not to follow or comply with the classroom or school rules.

Reactive vs. Proactive   Discipline policies, whether classroom or school-wide, are reactive in nature, and consequently, likely to be punitive. These policies assume a student knows appropriate behavior and chooses to break the rules anyway.

What is necessary then is for the 504 plan team or the IEP team to decide what the cause is of the student's inappropriate behavior—incompetence or noncompliance—and if they want to handle it in a reactive or proactive manner.

Fostering Appropriate Behavior

If a student is unskilled or incompetent, then the 504 plan, and in particular the IEP plan, must provide for the teaching of appropriate classroom and school behavior. Behavioral objectives and goals can be set with suggested strategies and activities to meet them. The IEP team can also put together a behavioral intervention plan (called a BIP in IEP jargon) which outlines how to teach appropriate behavior and the consequences for inappropriate behavior.

Involve your administrators! Keep in mind that it is very important to keep the school administration, particularly those people who handle discipline issues, informed about and involved in creating behavioral intervention plans for students with ADHD. These students won't experience behavior problems just in the classroom. Incidents may occur anywhere—on the playground, in the lunchroom, in the hallways, or in the classroom—so they need to be aware of the student's needs and difficulties.

Invite your administrators to your IEP or 504 plan meetings and provide them with copies of any behavioral accommodations or behavior intervention plans the student may be following.

Involve your parents! Parents can be crucial to providing follow-through to any behavior intervention plans that are created. They can also be helpful in reinforcing appropriate behavioral skills the student is learning in school by continuing activities and plans at home.

Inform all who need to know. Make sure other personnel are also informed of the student's behavioral needs and plans if they are affected by them. The student interacts with a variety of personnel every day, whether it's the bus driver, the lunch room attendants, the PE teacher, or the custodian. What works best for a student with ADHD is consistency in our expectations and behavior toward him—and with good communication that can be provided.

Use the sections on Adapting the Classroom Environment, pages 19-41, Developing and Improving Skills, pages 42-126, and Enlisting Parent Support, pages 193-214, to help you deal with this behavioral instruction.

In Reality

It would be ideal if every appropriate behavior could be taught, every BIP could be made and followed to the letter, and every person the student interacts with could be informed. Slip-ups and discrepancies will occur. Students won't cooperate and parents may not follow through.

So what do you do? The best you can. In some cases, that means you let the student face the reality of real life and the consequences of your school's and your teachers' classroom discipline policies. (The older a student is, the more I believe in this.) Once our students reach between 16 and 18 years of age, the "rules and policies" of real life—our laws—won't distinguish between a citizen with ADHD and one without.

What Students with ADHD Are Really Like

Anything but typical! ADHD has to be one of the most generic labels ever created to describe a condition that affects each student differently. For a student with learning disabilities, I can give another teacher or a parent general descriptors of what the student will do (most have reading, writing, or math types of problems) and what things might help. Not so for the student with ADHD. In all my years of teaching, I've yet to have any two students with ADHD display the same symptoms and behavior or react the same way to any strategies or methods I've tried.

Students with ADHD are also an enigma to the regular education teacher. Teachers find them very hard to understand. These students are seemingly very bright and articulate. Even in 2002, some teachers still view students with ADHD as "lazy" since they are often disorganized and don't complete their work, though they appear to have the ability to do so. Teachers believe that because the students are so smart, they should be able to pass. It doesn't help that these students have behaviors that antagonize teachers like closing their books too early when the teacher is going over things, spacing off during instruction, frequently forgetting their assignments in their lockers, or interrupting class with their impulsive behaviors.

Here are some quick snapshots of some of my students with ADHD to hopefully prepare you for the wide variation that exists.

Note: Although actual students are described below, their names have been changed.

Melany

Melany has the silent type of ADHD. She is very nice and quiet. She works slowly and gives you very few clues about what she is or isn't understanding. She takes medication to help her stay focused, but has to be monitored at home and by the school nurse to make sure she takes it.

In class, Melany appears to be working and to know what the assignment is. However, particularly for larger projects or papers, she'll often get started, but never turn in a finished assignment. She will tell you she'll "turn it in tomorrow," but that time usually doesn't come. She requires close monitoring of work completion and understanding of directions. Melany is also more comfortable if she is in a class with fewer students where she's more likely to interact with them and with the teacher.

Randy

Randy is a 15-year-old regular education student who I met while team teaching an English 9 class. He's one of those students we special educators meet in the course of working in the regular classroom. We often spot kids other than our "own" whose symptoms and needs parallel those of students already receiving such help.

Randy works very hard to pay attention. He's much more attentive in the morning than later in the day when he might be in a class where he and another student "feed off" of each other's distractible behavior (by afternoon, unmedicated attention deficit is hard to keep in check). Randy takes a long time to finish written assignments and take tests and quizzes. He focuses better and works more quickly and accurately when he can dictate answers to someone else or write his answers directly on a quiz paper.

Despite referral for some form of special help, Randy's parents have yet to consent. In particular, they prefer he not be in special education. Randy himself has requested extra help and he doesn't care if it's a 504 plan or an IEP. He doesn't want to fail and he's willing to put up with any perceived "harassment" from his peers. I tell him he's the smart one to know when he needs help and that he just needs more time or a different way to do things. I'm afraid Randy will get tired from all the effort he must put forth to stay attentive, to be enthusiastic, and to keep trying. I'm hoping at the start of the school year that an IEP or a 504 plan is in place for Randy.

Kyle

Kyle is a pure delight. He's bright, articulate, funny, and never hesitant to share his opinion. He is also typically ADHD-predominately hyperactive. You can tell easily when he hasn't had his morning dose and needs to be sent to the nurse. His Building and Trades teacher last year made a deal with him—if he hasn't taken his meds, he doesn't get on the bus to go build the house his class is constructing.

Kyle is great about asking for help (almost too much so). He'll let you know when things need to be slowed down for him or when he needs extra explanation (though we're working on volume control with him). He's highly motivated, very bright, and luckily, somewhat organized, although once in a while a locker check unearths a few past assignments.

Unfortunately, Kyle has few friends in or outside of school. His impulsivity and his overreaction to things at times make him appear immature to fellow students.

Nate

Nate is a 16-year-old sophomore. He's short for his age and acts immaturely. He has severe symptoms of ADHD even though he is on medication for it. For the past two years, he has been on several trials of different medications to see what helps his symptoms in addition to some psychological problems he is experiencing. One doctor has prescribed medication to deal with possible manic-depression in addition to medications for the attention deficit. Nate has trouble sitting still and focusing even when he is on medications.

Sometimes Nate is very tired and other times he is extremely restless. It has taken him four semesters to finish an individualized basic algebra class that most students can finish in two semesters. At one time in junior high, he was placed in a program for the behavior disordered and had an individual aide. Last year, he had a good two-thirds of a school year in my resource program until medications were changed.

At this point in time, I communicate with the school nurse, regular teachers, and Nate's parents frequently regarding his behavior in the classroom. Nate's IEP has also been adjusted to handle his wide swings in performance. Rather than holding him to credits for graduation like other regular students in the school, Nate will graduate based on meeting IEP goals that are relevant, practical, and realistic for him.

Some Guiding Principles

As I look back at what I've written about the diagnosis and treatment of students with ADHD and the descriptions of some of my students, it's clear that some basic principles guide everything I have found effective with these students. Whether I'm communicating with my students' parents, teaching the students appropriate behavior, or helping them to acquire academic skills, these guidelines prevail. For the purposes of an easy-to-use mnemonic, I call them the 8 C's.

The 8 C's of ADHD

Consideration Consider that each student with ADHD is different from another student with ADHD. Consider that whatever we do to help such students affects their emotional, social, and academic well-being.

Compromise Helping the student with ADHD requires a continuum of activities and strategies between home, school, and the child. Sometimes that requires compromise and an understanding of the student's life beyond the school day. It doesn't mean we don't try things, just that at times we have to adjust our expectations and make the best of the support we have.

Clarity Students with ADHD require clear explanations and directions whether they're steps for a math problem or a description of the kind of behavior we expect. Be as specific as possible in stating what you want.

Conciseness Along with clarity goes conciseness. Say what you want in as few words as possible. Remember, the student has an attention problem so you need to help him focus on what's important.

Consistency When we work with students with ADHD, we're really training and teaching them how to focus and what to focus on. Consistency in rules, expectations, and explanations helps take out the guesswork for them so they can focus and learn.

Consequences It's important to spell out for students with ADHD the consequences of good behavior, the consequences of inappropriate behavior, and the consequences of doing well or poorly on schoolwork. They don't have the problem solving skills to draw logical conclusions so we need to help make them clear.

Consensus Because working with a student with ADHD requires a multidisciplinary team, it's important to have consensus among team members. Each team member needs to understand and accept his or her role in helping the student do his best socially, emotionally, and academically.

Communication Helping the student with ADHD is an ongoing process from class to class, from class to playground, school to home, and back again. Keeping multidisciplinary team members and the parents informed of the student's progress makes for an extremely effective program.

How to Use *The ADHD Companion*

Like other books in LinguiSystems' Companion series, *The ADHD Companion* is a book of easy-to-use ideas and strategies. This resource can be consulted time after time as you make accommodations for your students with ADHD in and out of the classroom and as you help other teachers who also serve them. Working with the student with ADHD requires adjustments—minute by minute, hour by hour, day by day, situation by situation—so his learning environment and instructional modes are optimal for meeting his needs.

The following format is used to help you tailor instruction to fit the needs of your students with ADHD as they participate in the general curriculum.

Need
This statement describes a need that is unique to the student with ADHD. The statement describes the student's basic need within the instructional area and what teachers need to do, in general, to meet it.

Strategy Focus
This gives you the general target area for the instructional strategies that follow. The focus reflects a broad area of need experienced by most students with ADHD.

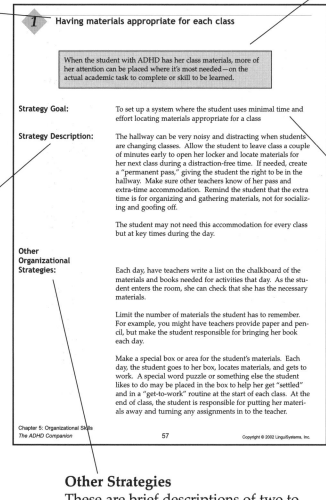

Strategy Description
This is like a lesson plan that models how to make adaptations in the classroom or other relevant situation. Because it is a strategy, it can be adapted and used multiple times in a variety of situations.

Strategy Goal
This is a specific statement of the goal this strategy is intended to meet. The strategy goals are phrased in a way that they may be used as actual IEP goals if desired.

Other Strategies
These are brief descriptions of two to three other strategies that might work to cover the same need. A variety of strategies are provided to meet the varied needs of your students.

Other chapters have been provided to help you while working with the student's parents and other professionals in your building. Those chapters include things like tips and handouts you can use with your multidisciplinary team to meet the student's academic, behavioral, and social needs.

Working with students with attention deficit is at once challenging and yet rewarding. With the help of the strategies and examples in this book, hopefully this task will be easier for you.

Every day, I treasure the moments when my students succeed, when I or their regular teachers have been able to focus and make the most of their efforts. I wish you the same success in your teaching and many rewards for your students.

Molly Lyle Brown

Chapter 1: Classroom Routines

Establishing consistent classroom routines is very important to meeting the needs of the student with attention deficit hyperactivity disorder (ADHD). We all know every student with ADHD is different. Some students take medication that may or may not help the accompanying distractibility and/or behavior problems, some need medication but don't or won't take it (or aren't allowed to), some have fantastic parent support, and with other students you do the best you can with the resources at hand.

No matter what the situation, routine and predictability in your classroom provide a safety net and a sense of comfort to your students with ADHD. Each day can seem as if it's totally brand new. Past experiences don't always carry over due to attention and memory problems. Having classroom routines helps alleviate students' anxiety over new situations and trying to keep up with their peers.

Establishing the right routine in your classroom involves a three-step process:

1. developing a consistent set of classroom rules
2. predicting and handling problem areas
3. accommodating for individual student needs

Though students may complain about what they perceive as "strictness" or about all the rules they have to follow in a classroom, they actually prefer knowing what's expected. For the student with ADHD, it takes the guesswork out of knowing what to do from one day to the next. It eliminates some of the disruptive "testing" behaviors students with ADHD exhibit when they don't know how to act in a situation.

- Choose a few classroom rules or "routines" you believe will create a "working" environment in your room. Your everyday classroom rules might look like the following.

Classroom Rules

1. Enter the room quietly.

2. Put your homework in the Homework Bin.

3. Get materials out for the day.

4. Do the Opening Activity.

5. Remain seated and quiet between all activities.

Notice that Rules #2 and #4 are reminders of routines that might exist in the room to facilitate students settling down and being organized for the day.

- Place a Homework Bin in a place students will see when entering and leaving the classroom. Having students put work in a Homework Bin eliminates the movement, noise, and shuffling around that happens when students pass in assignments. More importantly, students know exactly where homework is turned in and the bin prompts them so assignments don't go missing or accumulate in lockers.

- Start the day with an Opening Activity to establish a quiet atmosphere for work right from the beginning of the class period. A journal topic, question of the day, Daily Oral Language exercise for Language Arts class, or a review of math problems provided on an overhead projector may work well as an opening activity. With lights off or low and a short assignment to engage their attention, students tend to settle down. Meanwhile, you can take attendance, handle late work, and settle those who don't settle well without interrupting the day's plan.

- Be sure to post the rules on large posters and place them in the room for easy reference. Individual students, especially younger ones, may benefit from their own copies taped to their desks.

 ## Predicting and handling problem areas

No matter how well we try to anticipate students' needs during a particular lesson or activity, problems will occur. Students will get frustrated and give up or possibly act out. As much as you can, however, anticipate difficulties and have strategies for handling them so they interfere with instruction as little as possible. Better yet, try to structure what you're doing in class to completely avoid problems, if possible.

Here are some typical problem areas and some strategies you might use to deal with them:

- note-taking
- direction giving
- instruction
- restlessness and movement
- listening and paying attention
- partner or group work
- transitions between activities
- organization

Note-taking

Have copies available of notes you may want your students to copy from the chalkboard or overhead projector. Eye-hand coordination and attention problems can double the time it takes for a student with ADHD to complete such notes. Providing notes a student can follow along with or copy at her desk will lessen distractibility and frustration.

Another alternative is to provide guided notes for those who struggle to listen or write, or who don't identify key ideas very well. These notes can be in the form of a basic outline the student fills in or longer fill-in passages for the student to complete as she listens. (See Chapter 12: Writing, pages 172-187.)

Direction Giving

When giving directions, write them on the chalkboard or overhead projector first. Be sure to list the directions in a step-by-step manner so they are easy to follow.

---Example---

How to Complete Your United States Map

1. Color each state separately with colored pencils.
2. Try to use different colors for states in an area so each individual state is easy to see.
3. In blue or black ink, neatly write the name of each state in the middle of the state.
4. Put the map in your Social Studies folder when you are done.

Maps are due by 11:00.

- Orally go over the directions step-by-step. For students with more severe attention problems, write directions on a sheet of paper they can have at their desks to refer to.

- Show your students specific examples of what their work or project should look like when it is done.

- Set specific time limits for completing the assignment. Write the time on the chalkboard.

- Check student understanding after giving directions to the whole class. For students with listening or attending problems, have them paraphrase the directions.

Instruction

Vary your instructional methods each class period to keep students engaged. Use visual and auditory approaches simultaneously so you have the attention of all types of learners. Also vary the kind of instruction within a time period to keep students attentive and involved. For example, students could listen to a short passage read aloud in their science book. Then in pairs (e.g., with the person next to or directly behind them) have them find the main ideas of the passage. Pairs might verbalize or write the main ideas as notes.

For a hands-on activity, establish key stopping places in a story you're reading in class. Have students draw a scene from the story at each stopping place. The pictures then serve as a summary after the story is finished.

Restlessness and Movement

All students need to move at times and may appear restless or inattentive. Students with ADHD, in particular, need legitimate movement times. Build in purposeful physical breaks for students. For example, rather than circulating in the room to help students with math problems, a student might walk to you for help. Have an individual student desk next to yours for this purpose. Or during the assignment, call some students up one by one to check how they're doing. Remind students to leave their desks quietly and keep their hands to themselves.

- As long as students can handle the situation appropriately, let individual students pass back assignments, hand out materials, or take attendance to the office as ways of getting a physical break.

- A student may need a more isolated spot in the room in order to work. Allow that student to move to that area on her own when she recognizes her need for movement and a change of environment.

- Have a plan for how you'll handle excessive agitation and frustration from individual students while you're trying to teach. Establish a "get control plan" and a "get control area." For some students, it may work to have them step outside the room temporarily until they're ready to get back to work. A student might say, "I need a drink, Ms. Roberts" as a signal you agree upon for allowing her out of the room to get control.

- Sometimes a beanbag chair in a corner where the student can go can be quite calming. The fact that the beanbag chair "hugs" the student, so to speak, helps calm her down and lets her regain physical and emotional control. Even older students benefit from these strategies.

- Whatever you do, have an effective plan you and the student agree upon so times of restlessness or frustration don't become confrontational and disturbing to the rest of the class.

Listening and Paying Attention

- Establish consistent cues for getting your students' attention. You might use a sound signal like a soft bell, a clicker, or a consistent phrase like "It's Stop and Listen time." Then wait for students to become attentive. Don't "nag" or repeat yourself as students soon learn to tune out until they see you losing your patience.

- For some students, you may need to use proximity once in a while to get their attention. Move to where the inattentive student is as a subtle cue to pay attention. If necessary, add a quiet "Pay attention now" to get the student back on track.

- Students with ADHD may also appear daydreamy or quietly inattentive. Once you get to know these students, you'll be able to tell whether or not they are actually listening and will be able to ignore their seemingly "inattentive" behavior.

- Some students may need to handle an object quietly to sustain their attention. Playing with a paper clip, squeezing a small rubber ball, or twisting a plastic straw may calm their distractibility as long as they don't distract others. Older students often doodle and draw on their folders or papers.

Partner or Group Work

Use consistent partnering or grouping. To develop effective working relationships between students, especially those with ADHD or other disabilities, select the same students to partner or work in small groups each time. Join students whose abilities, attitudes, and work habits complement one another so both students are productive.

Partner or group work time may also be an opportunity for you to work more closely with one or two other students as their "partner" until they're ready for independent peer group work.

Transitions Between Activities

Plan how transitions will be made from one activity to another. Don't give students more than one instruction at a time. Be sure to allow students to finish what they're doing totally before making a transition. For the student needing extra time, discuss with her individually when to have her work done. For example, the student might finish in the resource room or be allowed to take work home to finish.

Organization

Having a "get organized" time at the beginning and end of the day can help many students with their daily transitions. It can especially help students who become unsettled when different or new things occur in their usual daily schedule or classroom routine. It is a time when they can review the events of the day before them, prepare for anything that's different in their routine, and get appropriate materials ready. At the end of the day, students can organize their materials and homework so they are prepared for what they'll need at home.

Some students with ADHD may need individual time to touch base with their special education teacher for extra organizational help. Or they may need extra time to go to their lockers at the end of the day to make sure work goes home. However it happens, having purposeful, planned time for organizing and preparing for transitions can be very beneficial for all students.

3 ⬥ Accommodating for individual student needs

Using what you know about your students' disabilities, how they handle class work, and how they interact with their peers, you can anticipate what accommodations or modifications they might need each day to succeed at a particular lesson or activity. Each student's needs must be considered individually on a regular basis.

Anticipating needs means asking questions about each student like, "Will Dan be able to work with a partner? Can Chris handle the cutting and drawing this project requires?" and "Will Raina be able to present her book report in front of the class like the others?" Asking such questions allows you to preplan and make adjustments ahead of time that will hopefully help lessons and activities go more smoothly.

When you have students in your classroom who have ADHD or other special needs, planning ahead will help you make accommodations and modifications for them. Such modifications can be made for means of instruction, class work and homework, testing and assessment, and the classroom environment. Because a supportive classroom environment is crucial for students with ADHD, it is covered in a section of its own. (See Chapter 3: The Classroom Environment, pages 38-41.) Typical modifications and accommodations for instruction, class work and homework, and testing and assessment are described below.

Means of Instruction

- Have easier, high-interest supplemental materials available, like easier novels and stories, workbooks for practice, and simplified maps.

- Use computer instruction to teach and reinforce concepts and skills.

- Teach to small groups as much as possible.

- Provide hands-on activities and practice for variety and interest.

- Let students work in pairs to help teach each other.

- Read textbooks and stories aloud while students follow along in individual copies.

- Vary means of instruction within a class period to maintain high interest. For example, students could view a videotape, complete an accompanying study guide, then pair with another student to complete and check answers.

- Invite guest speakers from your community or from within your own school. Students are usually more attentive to new people.

- Establish a daily instructional routine. For example, students could review homework or a recent lesson first, learn new material next, follow-up with a partner activity, and then complete individual work.

Class Work and Homework

- Provide homework or class work in the form of already prepared worksheets so the student doesn't face difficulties with copying and handwriting. Make sure questions and problems are easy to read with friendly type size, font, and ample space between items.

- Don't assign homework as long as the student is productive in class and understands concepts.

- Grade homework and class work on a pass/fail basis using established criteria and to reward students' good efforts.

- Give individual students extra time to complete assignments. However, agree on a reasonable and specific time for the assignment to be turned in. For example, a student with an IEP may be given one extra day for a lengthier assignment.

- Shorten assignments. Decide how much of the assignment a particular student really needs to do to show her understanding and mastery.

- Allow students to audiotape assignments instead of writing.

- Provide a work partner for a student who can write down the student's answers for her.

- Let students use the computer to word process assignments. Handwriting, spelling, and attention problems may be lessened through word processing.

Testing and Assessment Accommodations

- Let students write on tests and mark off their answers as they use them.

- Allow oral testing for a student with the classroom teacher or in the resource room.

- Allow for extended time on the same day or by breaking testing up over two or more days.

- Provide students with a study guide with sample questions so the student can rehearse test taking ahead of time and reduce her anxiety level.

- Create multiple choice or matching tests instead of fill ins, short answer, or essay questions.

- If fill-in questions are used on a test, provide a word bank for students to choose from.

- Read the test to small groups or individuals in another room or area.

- Allow the student to dictate answers instead of writing them.

- Enlarge print and create open white space around answers and between questions for easier reading.

- Modify grading criteria. For example, don't take off for spelling, neatness, or sentence structure unless it is what you're testing.

- Allow students to retake tests if you believe doing so will provide better and accurate results.

- Reduce the number of answer choices. For example, have three multiple choice answers instead of four.

- Reduce the number of test questions a student is required to answer compared to her peers.

- Modify or rewrite the test to create a more appropriate reading and language level.

- Grade tests on a pass/fail basis, or reduce the "weighting" of the test grade.

- On math tests, allow students to use a calculator, strategy or rule reminder cards (See Chapter 9: Mathematics, pages 127-139), or multiplication tables.

Your Daily Planning Routine

Establishing your own routine in regards to your students with disabilities can be a lifesaver in meeting their needs and also carrying out your other responsibilities. Teachers and other professionals who work with students with disabilities must be ultra-organized and proactive planners to ensure things go well in their classrooms.

You may want to develop a "to do" list that you can use each day to help you prepare. As you develop your list, make sure you include the following items along with any others you feel are important:

✓ Write the day's agenda in a consistent spot on the chalkboard.

✓ Make extra copies of notes, worksheets, and tests.

✓ Prepare guided notes or study guides.

✓ Adjust assignments for students needing accommodations (e.g., shorter amount of work, audiotape, tape recorder for dictating student).

✓ Locate and have alternative materials (e.g., audiotape, tape recorder, computer/software, alternative reading material) ready.

✓ Plan for transition times.

Make your own or have a printing store make To Do lists you can use regularly to check off what you need to do. Your list might look like the following.

Daily To Do List

❑ daily agenda

❑ extra copies

❑ guided notes/study guides

❑ assignments adjusted

❑ alternative materials

❑ transition times

You might also use the Unit Planning Sheet and Student Accommodation Sheet on pages 30 and 32 to help you meet the individual needs of your students. These planning tools help you look at your unit and lesson content, objectives, and skills as you plan individual accommodations within your classes.

Students' Daily Schedule

Your students' daily schedule will vary depending on whether you're responsible for students all day or for several classes like in elementary school, or for individual periods like in middle and high school. Whatever your teaching situation, you can establish a class-by-class schedule that establishes a routine that is particularly helpful for students with ADHD or other disabilities.

Your schedule may be similar to the following one that describes what happens from the moment students enter your classroom until class time is over.

---Example---

Class Schedule

1. Students check board for day's agenda and materials list.
2. Students retrieve needed materials from desk and/or designated storage areas.
3. Students complete Opening Activity. (See page 20.)
4. Go over the class agenda on the board.
5. Instructional time and activities.
6. Closing time including the following:

    ✓ fill in assignment notebooks
    ✓ review the next day's plan and expectations
    ✓ put materials away

Unit Planning Sheet

Student _____   Teacher _____

Class _____   Date(s) _____

Unit Title _____

Unit Objectives _____

_____

_____

Concepts and Skills _____

_____

_____

Day 1 Lesson	Activities
Day 2 Lesson	Activities
Day 3 Lesson	Activities
Day 4 Lesson	Activities
Day 5 Lesson	Activities

Unit Planning Sheet

Student __Amie__   Teacher __Brown__

Class __Math 7__   Date(s) __March 11-15__

Unit Title __Working with Geometric Figures__

Unit Objectives __will know different types of geometric figures, will compute area of geometric figures, will recognize units of measurement for area__

Concepts and Skills __area, units of measurement, understanding and using formulas__

Day 1 Lesson	Activities
Names of Geometric Figures	Discuss and have actual objects so students can handle and recognize features.
	Put label with figure's name on each object.

Day 2 Lesson	Activities
Dimensions of Geometric Figures	Review features and name figures.
	Overhead transparency drawings of figures for note-taking and labeling of sides, height, base, circumference, etc.

Day 3 Lesson	Activities
Units of Measurement	Make actual square inches to fill squares and rectangles.
	Color squares first, then glue to figures and label.
	Use figures tomorrow for formulas too.

Day 4 Lesson	Activities
Area Formulas	Overhead transparency figures with formulas for note-taking and discussion. Use figures from Lesson 3 and find area with partner.
	Overheads of figures with dimensions; class practice.

Day 5 Lesson	Activities
Individual Practice with Area Formulas	Worksheet to find areas of square, rectangles, circles
	Be ready for short quiz next day.

Student Accommodation Sheet

Student _____   Teacher _____

Class _____   Date(s) _____

Unit Title _____

	Activities	Accommodations Needed
Day 1		
Day 2		
Day 3		
Day 4		
Day 5		

Student Accommodation Sheet

Student __Amie__   Teacher __Brown__

Class __Math 7__   Date(s) __March 11-15__

Unit Title __Working with Geometric Figures__

	Activities	Accommodations Needed
Day 1	students handle objects and learn names	sheet with drawings and names for Amie to study
Day 2	notes on geometric figures	have note copy available for Amie to highlight and copy notes from
Day 3	cut and color squares and glue to figures	cut and color squares ahead of time; Amie can glue
Day 4	notes on area formulas partner activity with figures from Lesson 3 class practice with formulas	have note copy available for Amie to highlight and copy from partner Amie with Alyssa none
Day 5	worksheet on areas of squares, rectangles, and circles	make worksheet on just squares and rectangles for Amie quiz for her will cover just squares and rectangles

Chapter 2: Teacher and Class Selection

Unlike the student with a math disability, for example, a student with attention, impulsivity, and hyperactivity difficulties faces challenges the entire school day in every class and every situation. Consequently, choosing the kinds of teachers and classes the student has is extremely important. Selection should be focused on meeting these crucial objectives:

- creating an environment that nurtures and protects the student's self-esteem and emotional well-being
- providing consistency for the student through clear behavioral and classroom expectations
- adapting to the learning style and needs of the student
- helping the student learn self-control and self-management

Choosing a Teacher

A lot of thought and planning should go into selecting a teacher for the student with attention deficit hyperactivity disorder (ADHD). Teachers who are positive influences on these students usually have the following characteristics.

Enthusiasm The teacher is enthusiastic about kids and her subject matter and can spread this enthusiasm to her students.

Flexibility The teacher is willing to try new things to make learning and success possible for all students. A teacher who is flexible will make the accommodations needed by the student with ADHD.

Highly Organized A teacher who has a well-organized instructional style as well as an organized classroom environment provides the structure and consistency needed by students with ADHD.

Patience and Understanding It's important for the teacher to understand that the student with ADHD is not choosing to be "lazy" or disorganized—it is part of his disability. The student needs teachers who understand student needs and can provide individualized help.

Consistent Students with ADHD thrive in environments where rules and consequences are consistent and fair. The teacher should maintain good classroom control since students with ADHD can unknowingly mirror inappropriate behavior due to their impulsivity and weak social skills.

Attentive Not all students with ADHD exhibit hyperactivity or impulsivity. Some students' inattention may take the form of quiet and daydreamy behavior. The teacher should be attentive to the individual needs and progress of each student.

Good Instructional Skills An effective teacher provides both visual and auditory reminders to help all students learn and remember what to do. The teacher also uses a variety of instructional techniques to sustain student interest, but without so much variety that it makes class confusing for the student.

Communicative It's important for the teacher to be willing to take the time to keep others informed. Because the academic performance of a student with ADHD is consistently inconsistent, the student's parents and special education teacher need frequent updates on the student's progress. Also, since a student may misbehave in class, it's important to problem solve together to provide consequences for misbehavior as well as opportunities to learn appropriate behavior.

In choosing your students' teachers, use common sense and take advantage of those relationships and consistencies that have worked well for a student. For example, you may be able to create situations like the following.

- If a student is involved in a sport, the coach may also be a PE teacher or another content area teacher. Schedule the student in a class with his coach. It's sometimes amazing how much more productive a student can be when he needs to "prove himself" both on and off the field.

- For elementary students, keep the same teacher or core group of teachers from one year to the next, if possible.

- At the middle school and high school grade levels, it is sometimes possible to schedule a student with the same teacher for two class periods a day (unless the teacher needs a break from the student!) or from one semester to the next. For example, a student may be able to take a computer keyboarding class and a general business class from the same teacher.

- If students are in study halls, it may be possible to schedule a student into a study hall with a teacher he has during the day. That way, the student can get extra help and complete any unfinished assignments.

Choosing Classes

Choosing what the student takes is as important as who does the teaching. Several factors should be considered when choosing classes for your students.

Medication Needs Consider the effect that the student's medication needs will have on performance in a particular class. For example, you may be asking for disaster if you place a student in a woodworking class first thing in the morning when his morning medication hasn't kicked in yet.

Ask yourself questions like the following to guide your selection.

- When does the student take his medication?
- Will the student need to leave class to take medication?
- How will the fact that a student's medication may be wearing off or not be totally effective yet affect his class performance?

Time of Day It's a fact that a student may perform better at a particular kind of task at one time during the day compared to another. For example, one student may need the physical activity provided through a PE class at midday so his afternoon is calmer and more productive. Ask questions like the following when deciding when to schedule classes.

- When is the student more receptive to seat work?
- When does the student tend to become restless and more inattentive?
- When does the student seem to need more movement?

Need for Variety To sustain attention, some students with ADHD need variety in their schedules. One student may need a more structured morning with math, history, and reading classes followed by an afternoon filled with the hands-on activities that science and art classes can provide. Couple the student's need for variety with the times he performs best to put together an effective schedule.

Appropriateness Some classes may simply not be appropriate for a student with ADHD. For example, a class may have too many writing or physical demands for a student with additional coordination problems. Another class may move too quickly, even with accommodations, for the student to keep up without facing too much frustration.

A student's IEP or 504 plan allows you to create a realistic class selection and schedule to best meet his needs. Use questions like the following to guide your planning.

- What accommodations will the student need?
- What skill goals does the student have?
- For older students, what life and career goals does the student have?
- What course might be a reasonable substitution for another required course?
- Do any class requirements need to be waived for this particular student?

Creating a class schedule to meet the needs of the student will take flexibility and innovative thinking as well as realistic planning. With a proactive approach to planning for the student with ADHD, school can be a great experience for both the student and his teachers.

Chapter 3: The Classroom Environment

You are likely either a special education teacher or a regular education teacher providing accommodations for students with IEPs or 504 plans who have attention deficit hyperactivity disorder (ADHD) and/or other disabilities. Or perhaps you're a school administrator or a special education consultant helping to set up services, programs, and classrooms for students with ADHD. In today's schools, many students with a range of disabilities are educated in both special education classrooms and, through inclusion and 504 plans, in regular classrooms along with their peers.

In regular education classrooms in which I have worked as a team teacher with the regular education teacher, I have had as many as eight students at a time with special needs. Those students had learning disabilities, physical disabilities, ADHD, or autism. Along with their varied needs, one student had his own assistant. These are very ordinary situations for my role as a special educator in both special education and regular classrooms.

In other settings, more than one student may have an assistant in a classroom and some students may use assistive technological devices like a tape recorder or laptop computer to help facilitate attention, learning, and productivity in the classroom.

These typical scenarios, where multiple needs must be met simultaneously, greatly impact the environment you create within the classroom where you work. Planning for your students' needs requires consideration of these areas:

1. seating and work space arrangement
2. instructional materials and student supplies
3. placement of assistive technology

Seating and work space arrangement

Seating for Class Instruction

When you make up your daily seating chart for individual students, you'll need to keep several things in mind.

1. For students with ADHD, avoid seating them near high traffic areas like the pencil sharpener or door where they can be easily distracted.

   Also, consider seating these students in spots where they can see the chalkboard or overhead projector without turning or having to look over others.

2. Often a regular education teacher and special educator will work together in a classroom and move about frequently to help individual students. Put students who need extra help in easy-to-get-to areas. Seating these students in outer rows and the back row helps make it easier to respond more quickly to their needs.

3. If you have a student with physical disabilities who requires the use of a walker or wheelchair, or who brings along a computer on a cart for written work, seat the student where you or her assistant has easy access to her and where she doesn't inhibit access to other students in the classroom.

Space for Group Work

At times you'll need to work with smaller groups to supplement instruction or an assistant or a teacher in the room may want to work with just one or two students. Therefore, you will need to have an area separate from the class instruction area where you can have one or two small tables with chairs for students. It's ideal to have the table in an area that isn't distracting to other students who are working.

Space for Individual Work

Students with ADHD, in particular, may need alternative seating arrangements to help them manage distractibility during independent seat work. A student could pull her desk to a corner or other area, or sit in a study carrel when she is assigned independent work.

For a student assigned to read quietly, a beanbag chair on the floor can calm the student's movements so she can focus and read.

Students with ADHD are notorious for not having books and other classroom materials. You can choose to battle disorganization continually (and yes, students *do* need to be organized, but sometimes the need for a battle pales in comparison to other needs), or develop systems and strategies so students can be organized at least temporarily in your room. Eliminating as many sources of distractibility and frustration as you can means more time for actual instruction.

- For some students, you may want boxes, bins, or large baggies labeled with each student's name and containing the basic supplies for the classroom, including any books, folders, or workbooks.

- Another way to encourage better organization is to create a supply area near the teacher where a student can get pens, pencils, a book, or workbook, and leave "collateral" in exchange for items. Collateral could be things like a pen, a watch, or a book the student will need for another class. The student could check out the needed item and when she returns the item, she crosses off her name and the teacher gives back the item left as collateral.

- Establish a consistent area for turning in homework. A Homework Bin in an area near the door or close to the teacher's desk will remind students of work due and keep them from mixing assignments in with other papers in their folders and book bags. Taping a sample of the page due to the Homework Bin can help remind students what assignment they're looking for.

- Sometimes students are not assigned individual textbooks but may need to take a book home to finish work. Create a check-out area where students can sign out a book for the night.

- You will also need a place, like a filing cabinet or a separate shelf, to keep supplemental and modified materials for your students with special needs. The area needs to be easy to access so you can pull out what you need as you work with students of varying needs. Besides worksheets and workbooks, supplemental materials may include videotapes, audiotapes, or computer software.

Many students benefit from the use of assistive technology to accommodate for their disabilities or to enhance their interest in what they're learning. Assistive technology includes items like:

- computers
- tape recorders
- tape players
- headphones
- calculators
- other electronic tools for spelling, writing, and reading

You may need study carrels, counter space, or computer desks near electrical outlets on which to place assistive technology devices.

Visualize Your Classroom

Wherever you're teaching, visualize moving about the classroom working with students. Consider how your students learn, how they act, and what they need to stay as calm and focused as possible in the classroom.

Take your ideas and sketch the ideal room setup. With preplanning and some creative room arrangement, you can make your space an effective classroom environment.

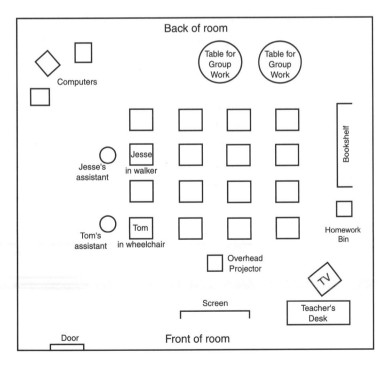

Chapter 4: Attention Skills

What, truly, is attention deficit hyperactivity disorder (ADHD)? It is a disability affecting a student's ability to appropriately focus attention on the task at hand. That task might be schoolwork, a conversation, and even a job responsibility. In addition, many students experience the added dimension of hyperactivity, usually worsening their attentional difficulties. Because of attention problems, the student may:

- focus too much, perseverate, or "get stuck"
- focus too little, rush, and be disorganized and sloppy
- become fatigued and frustrated
- appear lazy and disinterested
- annoy and distract others

Many significant areas of a student's life are affected by his inconsistencies in attentiveness:

- behavior and learning
- thinking and problem-solving skills
- social acceptance

To help these students, they need direct instruction in what to pay attention to, how to pay attention to it, and how much attention to pay at a given time.

The strategies and tips in this chapter will help maximize students' abilities to focus appropriately. Areas covered related to attention are listed below.

1. increasing visual attention
2. strengthening auditory attention and listening skills
3. paying attention to details
4. building interest and motivation
5. attending to directions
6. teaching self-monitoring
7. getting students' attention
8. accommodating attention difficulties

1 Increasing visual attention

> Students with ADHD may become distracted by too much visual information or stimuli. They need techniques to help them focus their visual attention appropriately.

Strategy Goal: To provide instructional materials the student is able to focus on appropriately

Strategy Description: Students deal with printed matter every day, whether it's a textbook, overhead transparency notes, or worksheets. Often these printed materials are way too visually cluttered for students to know what's most important to focus on.

Follow these guidelines when choosing or designing instructional materials for students to use:

1. **Use large type for emphasis.** When directions are presented in large type, students are more likely to pay attention. Also use larger type for headings on outlines or word webs or to accentuate vocabulary or terminology a student needs to know.

2. **Create "white space" as a visual break for students when they read.** For example, provide ample spacing between direction steps or question items on a test and their choices.

3. **Emphasize with color.** Use color highlighting markers to emphasize material on a worksheet or even in a textbook. For example, key vocabulary or concepts can be highlighted in pink in a textbook while core reading passages can be highlighted in yellow. Students who need highlighted texts can have one prepared by the core academic teacher and then checked out to them. Highlighted material should match questions and worksheets assigned so students can find needed information more easily.

Other Visual Attention Strategies: Students with ADHD find it difficult to divide their attention between reading, listening, watching, and writing while being expected to take notes. Provide the student with already prepared copies of notes. As the notes are reviewed, the student can simply listen or be instructed to underline or highlight the material as it is covered.

Regularly review with students how to read and/or visually attend to material for a given subject matter. For example, in science it's important to be able to follow captions, diagrams, and illustrated pictures. In math, students need to be able to follow operation signs, interpret graphs, and follow process steps. Try to isolate the material on the page when you discuss it. For example, you might enlarge and copy the diagram from the science book and then create an overhead transparency of it. Or, you might retype problems from the math book onto a page, adding more white space between problems so students can follow along better as you instruct.

2   Strengthening auditory attention and listening skills

Students with ADHD may have weak auditory and listening skills that affect their attention and work completion. They need direct instruction to practice and strengthen these skills.

Strategy Goal:

To provide the student with practice and activities for strengthening auditory and listening skills

Strategy Description:

Build in a listening component to your language arts or other skill/content instruction that can be used on a regular basis with your students. Listening activities might include things like:

- writing down a message
- writing a letter that is dictated
- practicing daily oral language from dictation
- solving the math word problem of the day
- answering the review question of the day
- answering the opinion question of the day

The dictation or activity can be tape recorded and repeated as necessary. For example, if the activity is a question of the day or math word problem of the day, the answer can also be recorded for students to listen to and check their work.

Other Listening and Auditory Strategies: When reviewing content material, have students repeat things aloud as a way to remember and study. For example, in a social studies class, students might be reviewing a process like how a bill becomes a law. They can list the steps on index cards and then get with a partner to repeat the steps to each other over and over until they memorize the information.

Some students have difficulty following conversations because of weak auditory and listening skills. Create audiotapes of made-up conversations for your students. Have students listen to the audiotapes and then summarize the gist of each conversation. Then encourage students to tape their own conversations. Remind them to signal by saying "It's your turn now" if they have trouble knowing when to alternate turns.

3 ◆ **Paying attention to details**

> Students with ADHD often overlook important details in what they read and do. They need explicit direction and instruction in which details to attend to in given activities.

Strategy Goal: To teach the student how to attend to specific details in assigned work

Strategy Description: When students are completing a reading assignment, they often don't understand which details are most important to attend to. To engage students in active reading and listening and to focus attention to detail, prepare study or question guides ahead of time for them. (See the example on the next page.)

Beside each question, you can also indicate which page or paragraph in which to find the answer. As you read aloud to students, take periodic breaks to allow them to answer the study guide questions and to review concepts with them.

```
Mammal Study Guide

1. What are the traits of a mammal?
   (page 52)


2. Name five common mammals.
   (page 54)


3. Draw a picture of one of the most
   unusual mammals shown in your
   book.  (page 55)


4. Describe how most mammals
   reproduce.  (page 56)
```

Other Attention-to-Detail Strategies:

Difficulty in paying attention to detail often results in poor work quality. When assigning work, make sure students understand what criteria to follow to create quality work. Specify things like:

- length of assignment when completed
- neatness
- spelling and handwriting criteria
- content to include
- due date for the assignment
- what materials and resources to use

Use grading rubrics frequently as guidelines for creating quality work as well as for final assignment grading. Rubrics should include quantity factors like how many math problems to do, how many pages to be typed, or how many characteristics to include in an assignment, report, or project. Quality factors like neatness, good grammar and punctuation, use of color, following directions, and accuracy of answers should also be included on any rubric. Be as specific as possible with the criteria you expect so students can meet expectations.

To enhance attention to visual detail, create or find already published hidden word and picture puzzles. Students can have fun while also strengthening their academic and attention skills. You might also allow students to play skill-related games on a computer to practice attending to details.

 4 Building interest and motivation

Students with ADHD are inconsistent in the amount of attention they pay to various classroom activities. They need activities and materials that help build their interest and motivation.

Strategy Goal: To provide the student with high-interest materials and activities that sustain his attention

Strategy Description: On a daily basis, provide a variety of activities or modalities for students to learn the same concept. Students with ADHD benefit from experiential learning. They are most interested when they can do, touch, examine, and take apart something.

A lesson plan with alternative high-interest activities might look like the following.

The Basics of Multiplication

Group Lesson—Teach the basic concept of multiplication to your students. Multiplication is taking a set of numbers and counting multiples of them. You might use the overhead projector or the chalkboard to draw sets of objects and then count to show how they become multiples of a number.

O O O   O O O
O O   O O

5   5

5 x 2 = 10

Individual Practice Alternatives—Allow students to choose from one of the following activities for a given length of time.

1. Color in sets of objects on a worksheet to show multiples of a number.

2. Count colored pegs into groups to make multiplication sets.

3. Let students work problems on a computer software program related to multiplication.

Other High-Interest Attention Strategies:

Allow students to work in groups or with partners on lesson activities. Create learning centers where students can work together to complete a variety of activities. Set parameters on how much students should accomplish at a given time.

When giving an assignment, break the task into two parts. Allow the student to choose which task to do first. He can complete the other one later.

Create activities that relate to students' own interests and experiences. When you first meet a class, survey what students' interests and hobbies are. Then, when possible, create activities related to their interests. For example, if a group of students is interested in racing cars, a race car-themed unit could be created for math class or language arts class.

5 ▸ Attending to directions

> Students with ADHD may have trouble attending to and then following directions. They need directions presented in easy-to-understand and high-interest ways to keep their attention.

Strategy Goal:

To provide the student with clear, concise directions he can attend to and easily follow

Strategy Description:

Always provide directions for all students both visually and auditorily. First put the step-by-step directions on the overhead projector or the chalkboard. Then point to the directions as you explain them. During your explanation, be sure to use clear language and a slow pace so students can follow you.

For younger students, put the directions on large poster paper they can refer to. Keep directions available for reference throughout the activity.

When a student asks to have directions repeated, have him consult the written steps and get back on track. You won't need to repeat the directions yourself. When teachers continually repeat directions, they create the trap of being the only one remembering and being responsible for the directions.

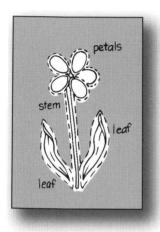

Flower Activity Directions
(Page 234 in lab book)

1. Color the picture of the flower parts.

2. Cut out the flower carefully.

3. Tape the parts of the flower together.

4. Label each flower part correctly.

5. Write your name on the back of your flower.

6. Put your flower on the shelf in the back of the room labeled with your class hour.

Other Direction-Following Strategies:

Provide individual copies of the directions for students. As students complete each step, they can cross it off and read what to do next. You can also provide the directions as a to-do checklist with boxes they can check off when they complete each step.

Give the student only as many steps at a time as he can manage without being overwhelmed. For example, in the activity above, one student may need to be given just the first three steps. When he finishes with those, he checks in with you to get the next three steps to complete the activity.

Have students repeat directions aloud to you to check their understanding.

Provide models of what a student should have when he completes an activity so he can check his work. Include demonstrations and examples as part of your directions, if they fit the activity.

> Students with ADHD may not know how to manage or sustain their attention. They need to learn to adjust their attention so it's appropriate for the task or situation.

Strategy Goal: To help the student develop a sense of pacing and time control when attending to tasks

Strategy Description: After giving an assignment, sit down with the student to review the assignment expectations and when it should be done. Help the student get started by clarifying directions and making sure he has all materials. Then, together, decide when to be finished.

Divide the assignment into steps or parts as needed and determine how long each step should take. Set a specific time with the student for the assignment to be done, acknowledging any accommodations he needs. Allow the student to work in a less distracting environment as long as he keeps pace with his work timeline.

Use a small sheet of paper to write down what you agree on. The student can keep the paper in front of him as a reminder.

---Example---

Math Assignment

Problems 1-5 by 10:10

Problems 6-10 by 10:30

Problems 11-15 by 10:50

Note: Clock faces can be used instead of the time for students who don't yet tell time.

Other Self-Monitoring Strategies: Use behavior management plans to encourage attentive behavior. For example, students can earn checkmarks or points during a given work period that they can then convert into incentives and rewards at the end of the week or day. A possible plan might look like the one on the next page.

Subject	Began On Time	Stayed On Task	Completed Assignment
Math			
Reading			
Language Arts			
Science			
Social Studies			

Don't hesitate to use timers or clocks to help students sustain attention and concentration. If a student needs to increase his attention span to 10 minutes, use a timer to gradually lengthen the time span. Encourage the student to work and stay attentive until the timer goes off.

Getting students' attention

> Students with ADHD may have varying levels of attention throughout a class period and the school day. They need frequent reminders to get back on task and pay attention.

Strategy Goal: To bring the student's attention back to the activity at hand and involve him actively

Strategy Description: However you bring a student's attention back to a lesson, it is important to be low-key and subtle. The technique you use to get the student's attention should not affect other students' involvement, and the student himself should not be embarrassed or made to feel he has "misbehaved." Techniques like the following may work to regain the student's attention.

1. **Proximity**—Move closer to the student even if you're conducting a class discussion. The student will hear you better and likely get back on track.

2. **Eye contact**—Before giving directions or talking to the student, make sure to establish eye contact.

3. **Simple language**—Use clear, assertive language for the message. Tell the student with a minimum of words what you want him to do.

4. **Touch**—Sometimes a simple hand on a shoulder can calm a student and get him back on track.

Other Attention-Getting Strategies: Use the student's name when trying to redirect his attention. This puts the student "on notice," so to speak, for being responsible for what's going on and should help direct attention appropriately.

Some students may need a mental break to regain and sustain their attention again. Allow the student to get a drink outside the room or to run an errand to the office. Or think of a different activity the student could do for a few minutes that changes the nature of the task he's doing or the environment or setting he's in. A short change can work wonders to bring the student back to task rather than having the student sit, get frustrated, and quit work altogether.

 ## Accommodating attention difficulties

> Many factors affect how well the student with ADHD can pay attention. He may need several classroom accommodations to help him attend and to perform well in class.

Strategy Goal: To provide the student with strategies that enhance classroom performance

Strategy Description: One of the main academic areas where a student may need accommodations is in the assessment of learning. This refers to testing and quizzing types of activities. If possible, don't "test" students' attention spans. These alternatives may help.

1. Avoid timed tests. Allow the student extra time to complete tests or to complete testing over more than one test session.

2. Don't use scantron sheets (i.e., bubble answer sheets). Students with ADHD easily lose concentration and can get off on numbers. They can also get frustrated with marking correct answers and erasing when they want to change answers.

3. Provide alternative testing and quizzing methods. Let students take oral tests where they discuss key concepts and ideas with you during a conference instead. Allow students to dictate answers to you or another student so their attention span doesn't interfere with their ability to think, process, and write answers.

4. Consider using portfolio activities instead to show the student's progress over time in a skill area.

Other Accommodation Strategies:

So students learn how to be attentive, seat them near good role models and away from distractions. They're less likely to act out or be inattentive around students with good behavior and work habits.

Use scheduling to take advantage of students' attention spans. Schedule classes with high interest for the student when you know his attention level is waning. For students on medication, schedule classes based on when their medications are very effective or when they're wearing off. (See Chapter 2: Teacher and Class Selection, pages 34-37, for additional scheduling tips.)

Ascertain whether a student's fiddling with an object or daydreaming is truly inattentive behavior. Some students need to handle an object (as long as it doesn't make noise or distract others) to channel their excess energy. Some students may also have their heads down or be looking somewhere else, but actually be listening very closely to you. It's their way of controlling their distractibility. You'll know how much they're really paying attention depending on how well they participate in class discussion and do on tests and quizzes.

Chapter 5: Organizational Skills

Neat, orderly, sequential, on-time, organized. Do these sound like impossible expectations for the student with attention deficit hyperactivity disorder (ADHD)? Not at all, but these students often experience academic failure due to organizational problems that interfere with acquiring new skills and completing work. These students have the intelligence and overall academic ability needed, but common behaviors like forgetting books and materials and misplacing completed assignments jeopardize academic success. To succeed in the classroom, they need more direct instruction and practice in learning skills that help them to be organized.

The strategies and tips in this chapter will help the student with ADHD learn organizational skills to help her achieve maximum success in the classroom. Organizational areas covered are listed below.

1. having materials appropriate for each class
2. having materials needed for homework
3. keeping materials neat and orderly
4. turning in assignments
5. using an assignment notebook for organization and communication
6. using a daily planner
7. creating a student schedule that enhances organization
8. setting up an organizational routine at home

Having materials appropriate for each class

> When the student with ADHD has her class materials, more of
> her attention can be placed where it's most needed—on the
> actual academic task to complete or skill to be learned.

Strategy Goal: To set up a system where the student uses minimal time and effort locating materials appropriate for a class

Strategy Description: The hallway can be very noisy and distracting when students are changing classes. Allow the student to leave class a couple of minutes early to open her locker and locate materials for her next class during a distraction-free time. If needed, create a "permanent pass," giving the student the right to be in the hallway. Make sure other teachers know of her pass and extra-time accommodation. Remind the student that the extra time is for organizing and gathering materials, not for socializing and goofing off.

The student may not need this accommodation for every class but at key times during the day.

Other Organizational Strategies: Each day, have teachers write a list on the chalkboard of the materials and books needed for activities that day. As the student enters the room, she can check that she has the necessary materials.

Limit the number of materials the student has to remember. For example, you might have teachers provide paper and pencil, but make the student responsible for bringing her book each day.

Make a special box or area for the student's materials. Each day, the student goes to her box, locates materials, and gets to work. A special word puzzle or something else the student likes to do may be placed in the box to help her get "settled" and in a "get-to-work" routine at the start of each class. At the end of class, the student is responsible for putting her materials away and turning any assignments in to the teacher.

◆2 Having materials needed for homework

> Students with ADHD often have trouble transporting assignments to and from home along with the materials to complete them.

Strategy Goal: To have the student develop the habit of gathering materials needed for homework

Strategy Description: Make a homework sheet for the student to keep in a central location in a three-ring notebook or zippered notebook. The homework sheet can include a space for listing the assignment as well as which book to take home. Individualize the sheet to reflect the student's exact materials. The student can then check the homework sheet before leaving for the day. An optional completion category can be added to the sheet.

Homework Sheet			
Subject	Assignment	Materials Needed	Completed
Math	pages 215-216; Do odd numbered problems.	☐ calculator ☐ Math workbook ☑ Math textbook ☐ worksheet	
Biology	page 108; Color and label flower parts.	☑ lab book ☐ Biology textbook ☐ worksheet	

Other Organizational Strategies: Establish an end-of-day checkpoint to ensure that the student has materials and books ready to take home. For example, the student could be allowed to go to her locker five minutes early to get organized for home or to meet with her special education teacher to see that she has the correct materials.

Depending on the severity of organizational problems, you may want to check out double sets of books to the student with one set to leave at home. Also encourage the parents to provide double sets of materials, like a calculator, paper, and colored pencils. Then the student is responsible only for knowing the assignment until she's ready to take on the added responsibility of remembering the necessary materials.

 3   **Keeping materials neat and orderly**

> When a student with ADHD carries her materials from class to class, she needs a system to help her easily remember where to find needed materials.

Strategy Goal: To create an organizational system that keeps the student's materials neat, orderly, and readily available

Strategy Description: Purchase, or have the student purchase, book covers and folders of matching colors or designs. Folders can have pockets for paper, assignments, and a pen or pencil for each class. Have the student memorize what colors go with which class. For example, the student might say to herself, "I need to get my red materials for Math and my blue materials for Spanish."

At the end of the week, have the student check her locker to make sure it's clutter free and matching materials are together. Some students may initially need a teacher to help with locker checks and clean-ups.

Other Organizational Strategies: Have the student keep two different colored three-subject notebooks, one for morning classes and one for afternoon classes. That way the student is looking for only one particular thing in her locker or desk. Having pockets available in each section may also help the student keep assignments for each class or subject in one place.

Build in a few minutes at the end of each class for the student to organize her materials. If possible, encourage the teacher to establish this routine for the entire class. The teacher can circulate around the room and check that students have placed materials where they belong.

Allow the student to carry a backpack or book bag from one class to the other so materials for an extended period of time are with her. Partway through the day, the student can exchange morning materials for afternoon materials.

 ## 4 Turning in assignments

> The student with ADHD needs a consistent routine of where and to whom an assignment is turned in to ensure it gets where it's supposed to go.

Strategy Goal: To develop a predictable routine for the student to follow when turning in assignments

Strategy Description: Create one central location for the student to turn in work. Options might include:

- a personalized, decorated box kept on a shelf
- a file folder labeled with the student's name and kept at the teacher's desk or another predictable location
- a hanging folder on the side of the teacher's desk

Other Organizational Strategies: If a student is working in a study carrel or another isolated area, establish a hand-in spot within the area. For example, place a bin in the carrel for completed work.

Sometimes an assignment doesn't get turned in because it isn't completely done. The student holds onto it, intending to finish it, but then forgets. Create a predictable routine for handling incomplete assignments too. For example, take the work the student does have done so she has some credit for the assignment, and have her turn in the rest of the assignment later. Make sure the student records what else she needs to do in an assignment notebook or on a sheet of paper.

5 Using an assignment notebook for organization and communication

> Students with ADHD need help knowing what information to include for assignments and also in recording them legibly.

Strategy Goal: To teach the student how to use an assignment notebook for organization and communication

Strategy Description: Keep the use of an assignment notebook as simplified as possible for the student. Have the student develop some short words, symbols, or abbreviations to use in recording assignments. She might develop a list like the following.

---Example---

Pg. = page
Sec. = section
Prob. = problems
?s = questions
Lab
Quiz
Test
NA = no assignment

At the beginning of each week, have the student date each page in her assignment notebook and list her subjects (if not already done so). Have the student record something for each subject, even if it's NA (no assignment) for the day, so it becomes a habit.

Other Organizational Strategies:

Use the assignment notebook as a once-a-week parent communication log about positive events that have occurred that week. The parent can see how many times the student was able to successfully record assignments, as well as learn about anything else that went well, like a good test score or all assignments turned in. Sharing the assignment notebook becomes a way for the parent and child to communicate about school on a regular basis. The parent can sign off that he's seen the notebook and also ask any questions or communicate any concerns that need to be discussed or clarified.

Create incentives for the student who succeeds in recording assignments for a set time period. For example, if the student manages for two days in a row, she might watch a favorite video.

Instead of an assignment notebook, have older students, particularly those going on to post-secondary school, learn how to use a daily planner. As young adults, they will be juggling school, work, and social activities and responsibilities and will need to develop personal organizational systems to help themselves throughout their lives.

6 **Using a daily planner**

> Good time management is a skill that is elusive to even the best of students. Students with ADHD, in particular, need to look over a whole day's plan to decide how to meet their daily commitments.

Strategy Goal: To help the student learn to use and maintain a daily planner as an organizational tool for life

Strategy Description: Make or have the student buy a daily planner with pages that cover a single day or week at a glance. Design an individualized one, if at all possible. Each day might include a section for Before School, School, After School, and Evening. Highlight in color those activities that take priority for the day.

Monday, January 21st		After School	
Before School		3:00	*Soccer 3:15-5:30*
7:00		4:00	
School		5:00	
8:00		*Evening*	
9:00		6:00	*Work 6-8:30*
10:00	WW1 project due.	7:00	
11:00		8:00	
12:00		9:00	
1:00		10:00	
2:00			

Other Organizational Strategies:

Planning one's day requires knowing how long certain tasks might take. Help the student learn how to estimate time needed. Together, make a list of things the student needs to accomplish on a regular basis including job, sports, and leisure activities. Allot an amount of time to each activity. Then have the student refer to the list when filling out her daily planner.

─Example─

Math homework—45 minutes
Spelling—10 minutes
Chores—30 minutes
Soccer practice—2 hours

Teach by example. While your students look over their daily planners, review your own. Share any simple strategies you've learned, as well as any learning-from-experience situations you've had in attempting to get everything done (like over-scheduling yourself!).

A daily planner can double as a diary or journal. Encourage students to write down favorite activities they did each day or how they felt when something happened. Making the planner a part of the student's in-school and out-of-school life can make it a valuable part of the student's everyday routine.

7   **Creating a student schedule that enhances organization**

> Students with ADHD need frequent, and in some cases, daily instruction and practice in getting and staying organized.

Strategy Goal: To create a daily schedule that helps the student get and stay organized

Strategy Description: Look over the student's past organizational behavior and decide when and how the student becomes disorganized. Is the student organized in the morning, but losing things by midday? Does homework go undone because the student leaves for the day with incorrect materials or no materials at all?

Create a schedule to practice and apply organizational skills. Depending on the extent of disorganization, a student may need one or more of the following suggested checkpoints. As students master organizational skills, the number of checkpoints can be decreased.

Beginning of the Day Checkpoint—Have the student meet with you at least 15 minutes before the day begins. Together, check with the student that she has paper, pencil/pen, assignments, and any other necessary materials. If she has what she needs for part of the day, review what materials she'll need for the rest of the day and when she should get them.

Midday Organization Checkpoint—You may need to schedule a few minutes right before or immediately after lunch to check in with the student. Or, if possible, have the student's teacher spend a few minutes with her before lunch to help with organization for afternoon classes.

End-of-Day Checkpoint—Sometime prior to the student leaving for the day, check with her that she has the materials and assignments that need to go home. If you have frequent communication with parents, send home information about the student's evening assignments.

Note: At my high school, we have Learning Labs which are small, structured times that replace assigned study halls. Students get extra academic help as well as help with study and organizational skills. It has worked extremely well for my students to have a Learning Lab at the very beginning of the day or at the very end, depending on their organizational needs.

Other Organizational Strategies:

Before the beginning of each semester, look over the student's schedule and adjust it to meet her organizational, learning, and attention needs. For example, if the student needs a midday checkpoint, choose a class and instructor combination that facilitates such a checkpoint.

Encourage the student's teachers to reward organizational efforts. For example, let the student earn a point a day for coming to class prepared. Add the points to assignment grades or exchange them for an extra treat or privilege.

8 Setting up an organizational routine at home

Students with ADHD need help with organization even beyond the school day. Many times they will have homework and will need help developing the habit of getting it completed on a regular basis.

Strategy Goal:

To help the student develop at-home routines to aid organization and work completion

Strategy Description:

It would be ideal for the student with ADHD to have accommodations that help eliminate "homework." However, many times, even with a reduction in length of assignments, the students will need to work outside of class.

Set up a predictable routine of homework. Have one or two teachers of subjects where the student most often has outside work make a weekly schedule of assignments, including the accommodations. Keep a schedule at school and send one home to the parents. Encourage the parents to establish a study area for the student as well as a consistent work time.

If possible, provide the parents with a second set of books or materials for the student to keep at home to complete these assignments.

Other Organizational Strategies:

After doing work at home, the student should put work and materials in a consistent spot. For example, have the student and/or parents check that things have been put in a book bag so things get returned to school.

Encourage the parents to have a daily work time even if there is no assignment. For example, if there isn't an assignment on a particular day, the student might read or practice math skills on the computer. Work time can earn the student extra privileges at home. This way the student develops the habit of being prepared and working every day.

If the student takes medication, have parents evaluate, with the help of the doctor, the effect of medication on the student's behavior in the evening. Some medications wear off by evening or can't be given too late as they interfere with sleep. Sometimes parents don't require the student to take medication to cover the evening time period. Have parents evaluate what's in the student's best academic and behavioral interest.

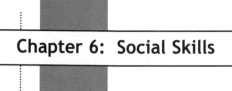

Chapter 6: Social Skills

Not every student with attention deficit hyperactivity disorder (ADHD) exhibits a level of impulsivity and aggressiveness that interferes with the ability to get along with others. However, enough of these students face the unfortunate consequences of weak social skills—frustration and anger, rejection by peers, loneliness, and low self-esteem—that those skills must be developed and strengthened. These students need direct instruction in social skill areas that many students pick up naturally on their own.

The strategies and activities in this chapter will help students with ADHD acquire social skills that will help them interact positively with those around them. Social skill areas addressed are listed below.

1. following instructions and rules
2. working cooperatively with others
3. taking turns and playing cooperatively
4. expressing ideas and feelings appropriately
5. predicting consequences of words or actions
6. coping with new situations
7. adapting language and behavior to various situations
8. interpreting and using social language
9. applying problem-solving techniques
10. initiating social interactions
11. using appropriate assertiveness
12. controlling voice volume
13. understanding peer reactions to inappropriate behavior
14. showing respect for peers' ideas and feelings
15. controlling topic perseveration

1 Following instructions and rules

> Students with ADHD may process information slowly and have gaps in understanding because of inattention. Consequently, they need rules and directions broken down into manageable chunks to help them remember.

Strategy Goal: To provide the student with instructions and rules in amounts and ways he can remember them

Strategy Description: Keep a stack of small index cards available for writing down instructions. Any time you give instructions, state each one in as few words as possible. Put each instruction on a separate index card, numbering each one. The student can then line the instructions up on his desk to help him remember as he works to complete a task. You may want to tape the cards to the desk to help the student keep them in order and in place.

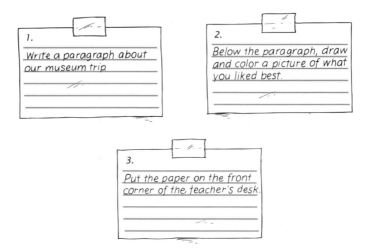

Other Social Skills Strategies: Any time you give instructions for an activity or assignment, present the information both verbally and in writing. You might have a couple of students restate the directions as a way of checking everyone's understanding.

Encourage parents to use the same kinds of strategies at home. For example, if the student helps in the kitchen, give him a written list, like wipe the table with a wet cloth, load the dishwasher, and rinse out the sink.

Have the student do listening activities frequently to boost listening attention. Strengthening the student's listening skills will help him improve his skills in following rules and directions.

 ## 2 Working cooperatively with others

Students with ADHD need clear rules and guidelines for behavior when they work together with other students. They also need help focusing on the task to be completed.

Strategy Goal:

To help the student acquire appropriate behavior so he can work cooperatively with other students

Strategy Description:

Allow students to work in pairs on a regular basis. For example, have students work together to complete end-of-chapter review questions for a history assignment.

Keep the same pairs each time so the student with ADHD is comfortable with the other student and can focus on the work.

Also allow the student to work in a spot that lessens the distraction that results from students working together (e.g., back corner of a room, outside in the hall, in the library).

Other Social Skills Strategies:

Provide a short checklist of what the pair should accomplish by the time they are done. This type of reminder can help the student stay on task.

Divide up the work ahead of time to avoid any conflicts over unfair workloads. For example, for a vocabulary assignment, one student could look up word meanings while the other student writes them down. Be sure to provide for any accommodations the student might need in this situation.

Remind students of expected behaviors each time they work together. Also write the specific time to be done and the place to hand in the work on the chalkboard to ensure they understand directions and stay on task.

 3 ◆ **Taking turns and playing cooperatively**

Students with impulsivity and aggressiveness associated with ADHD may have difficulty getting along with others in play situations. They need clear rules and structured play situations to be able to play cooperatively.

Strategy Goal:

To provide clear behavioral rules and a structured play situation to facilitate cooperative play

Strategy Description:

As you teach the student to play cooperatively with others, you may need to monitor his behavior closely. Make an At Play card that lists the behaviors you're looking for. Go over the behaviors with the student. Then periodically during play, record observations of those behaviors. Playing cooperatively can earn the student an opportunity to play another time or to earn some other incentive.

Name _____

At Play

Behavior	Yes	No
Shared with others	☐	☐
Put equipment, toys, or game away	☐	☐
Waited turn	☐	☐
Got along with others	☐	☐

Other Comments: _____

_____

**Other Social
Skills Strategies:**   Set up play situations that the student can be successful with. For example, a student may not be able to sit long enough to play a board game, but he could do a computer game with another student.

Have the student's gym or PE teacher work on the same play behaviors with the student. The student will be able to continue strengthening his social interaction skills and gain more peer acceptance.

 4   Expressing ideas and feelings appropriately

> The student with ADHD has ideas and feelings about many things. He needs to learn the words to describe these ideas and feelings and the appropriate ways to do so.

Strategy Goal: To give the student the appropriate words and manners for expressing ideas and feelings

Strategy Description: Sometimes the impulsivity of a student with ADHD can cause him to express himself inappropriately or in a loud, insensitive manner.

Don't hesitate to provide immediate feedback to the student about how he's coming across to you or someone else. He doesn't pick up on the cues himself, so he needs on-the-spot instruction and feedback as situations occur.

Student: "The Mets suck this year! They're all lousy players!"

Teacher Feedback: "Let's think about how you're coming across to someone else. How do you think someone would feel if he's a Mets fan? What's a better way to say the same thing?"

Student: "The Mets aren't doing very well this year. No one can hit. I like the Red Sox better."

Other Social Skills Strategies:

Make sure students also express themselves appropriately in writing. Allow students plenty of opportunity to write opinion papers and paragraphs. Encourage them to support their ideas with facts and examples rather than abrasive, emotionally-laden comments.

We've all heard the advice, "If you can't say anything nice, don't say anything at all." Use a similar guideline with the student with ADHD. Help him realize that if he can't say something in a nice (i.e., kind, sensitive, respectful) way, then he shouldn't say anything at all. If a student starts to express himself insensitively, stop him and tell him he can give his opinion when he's ready to do so in a respectful manner.

5 Predicting consequences of words or actions

> Students with ADHD need to learn higher degrees of self-control than other students. They need to learn how to predict consequences before they say or do anything.

Strategy Goal:　To provide the student with self-control techniques that help him predict consequences of behavior before he speaks or acts

Strategy Description:　Part of self-control is not only considering the consequences to oneself as the result of an action, but also empathizing with how others might feel or react.

Teach the student a technique that requires him to literally stop and think a few minutes before doing something. A technique like the following might work. Help the student practice and rehearse the technique with situations that are typical of what he finds himself dealing with.

Example

Think　Ask yourself, "What am I thinking of doing or saying? Why?"

Predict　Answer these questions in your mind, "What might happen to me? How might the other person feel or what might he do?"

Do　Do what's best for you and the other people in the situation.

Other Social Skills Strategies:　Emphasize empathy as a matter of routine in your classroom. For example, if you've directed the students to work quietly, ask them, "What happens if we become noisy?" (Other students can't think and do their work well.) Or if students have been told to put art materials away and lids on markers, ask, "What happens when we take care of materials properly?" (We have them in good shape to use the next time.)

Use your literature materials to help students develop empathy in real life. When reading, ask questions like, "How do you think _____ feels?" or "How will _____ feel if _____ does that?"

6 ◆ Coping with new situations

> Students with ADHD need to be prepared for changes in routines
> and activities as well as other unexpected situations. If the student
> can mentally prepare for changes, he will experience less anxiety
> and his behavior will likely be more appropriate.

Strategy Goal:

To help the student develop coping strategies for unfamiliar
and unexpected situations

Strategy Description:

Preferably the day before a change in activity or routine,
discuss the change with the student. If it's an activity that
affects the schedule for the day, like a special speaker in the
auditorium or a school field trip, go over the changes with
the student. Provide a written copy of the schedule change
or have the student copy it.

Make sure the student understands and is able to follow the
changes, and also knows what behaviors are expected during
the new situation. Allow him to ask lots of questions so he
becomes comfortable with the new situation.

**Other Social
Skills Strategies:**

For unexpected situations, like a fire drill or tornado warning,
create a buddy system. Students get with their buddy and go
to the appropriate spot. With a buddy, the student will feel
less anxious and have a good role model for appropriate
behavior during this time.

Frequently role-play handling unexpected situations as a
way of practicing problem-solving skills. Give the student a
hypothetical situation and ask him what he'd do and how he'd
act. Praise his thoughtful decision making.

Encourage teachers to familiarize all students with any
changes in routine and the behavioral expectations for new
activities. All students can benefit from specific descriptions
of expectations, and as a result, activities are likely to go
better.

Adapting language and behavior to various situations

> The student with ADHD may need reminders of "where he is"
> so he knows the appropriate language for the situation.

Strategy Goal: To help the student learn and use language acceptable to the situation

Strategy Description: Ask the student if we use the same language or talk the same way everywhere we go. Develop a list of differences for several common situations and discuss them and why the differences exist. Also discuss the consequences if you use language inappropriate to a situation. Consider situations like playing on the playground, eating in the lunchroom, working on a job, or going to a movie.

---Example---

On the Playground

Friendly teasing is allowed.
No swearing.
Louder voices are okay.

At Work

Friendly teasing is okay if it doesn't interfere with work.
No swearing.
Use a respectful, polite tone with your boss, customers, and co-workers.

Other Social Skills Strategies: Make sure students clearly understand your classroom rules for appropriate language use from the very first day of class. Display the rules on a large poster for easy reference if your students need reminding.

With younger students, use favorite characters from stories or short books. Have them role-play how a character might speak in another situation. How would Goldilocks act if she waited on a customer at McDonald's? How would Winnie the Pooh and Eeyore act and talk if they went to see a new movie at the theater?

In some unstructured situations, students may need frequent monitoring and reminding so they talk appropriately. For example, you might talk with your student's gym teacher, art teacher, or wood shop teacher if a student needs direct instruction regarding language.

 Interpreting and using social language

> The student with ADHD may not fit in with his peers because he doesn't use or understand their social language. He needs help interpreting slang or figurative language.

Strategy Goal: To make the student aware of current and common slang and figures of speech

Strategy Description: Clip out and post comic strips that illustrate characters using slang or figures of speech. Strips like "Beetle Bailey," "Funky Winkerbean," "For Better or for Worse," and "Sally Forth" often use such language for humorous effect. You may want to follow a particular strip with a student, using it for fun as well as learning purposes.

Other Social Skills Strategies: Several publishing companies produce games and workbooks for developing social language. Use these materials as part of the student's language arts curriculum. For example, Fridays could be the day the student and/or class works on social language skills like slang and figures of speech. Using games also allows students to have social interaction and practice other skills.

Whenever you're reading stories or books that use slang or figures of speech, discuss examples as they occur. You may want to keep a running list on the board, adding to it as students discover other examples.

Understanding slang and figures of speech is easier if you have a well-developed vocabulary, particularly knowledge of the multiple meanings of many words. Have the student do frequent vocabulary practice and exercises to boost his vocabulary knowledge.

 9 **Applying problem-solving techniques**

Students with ADHD, and hyperactivity in particular, may tend to act now and think later when handling problems. These students need a step-by-step process that decreases impulsivity and leads to successful problem solving.

Strategy Goal: To help the student develop a technique for problem solving that involves stopping and thinking through a situation

Strategy Description: Make a card reminder the student can keep in a notebook for reference when problem situations arise. The card may include steps like the following. Let students create their own strategy names to help them remember.

Slow Down and Think!

Step 1: Identify the problem.

Step 2: Decide how you feel about it.

Step 3: Think of two ways to handle the problem.

Step 4: Predict how each way might turn out.

Step 5: Decide if anyone else needs to help you.

Step 6: Solve it!

**Other Social
Skills Strategies:**
Routinely give the student hypothetical, realistic situations to practice his problem solving technique. In this way the student rehearses behavior before actually handling a problem.

Students sometimes need to remove themselves from a situation in order to think through how to solve it without distraction. If the student is at school, provide a separate spot in the room or allow the student to step out into the hall for a few minutes.

 ## 10 Initiating social interactions

> Students with ADHD have the same desire as other students to interact socially with their peers. Many times, they need to be given ways to appropriately begin or join in the interaction.

Strategy Goal:
To help the student learn and apply social interaction skills like conversation starters and how to greet someone

Strategy Description:
Cut out pictures or use photographs of everyday situations like children at a playground, a fisherman catching a fish, a boy playing a computer game, or a teenager washing a car. Choose age-appropriate pictures and include examples from school, home, work, and leisure activities.

Ask the student to react to what he sees in the picture, interpreting the situation and giving you details about what's happening. Then ask the student how he might interact with the person in the picture. You can pretend to be the person in the picture while the student role-plays what he'd do and say.

Student: Hi, it's sure a nice day for being outside.

Car washer: Hi, it sure is.

Student: Is that your car?

Car washer: No, it's my dad's, but sometimes I get to drive it.

Student: Cool! Would you like some help?

Car washer: Sure, just grab that other sponge.

Other Social Skills Strategies:

Students with ADHD also need to be encouraged to participate in after school clubs, sports, and other activities. Suggest clubs, sports, and activities where you know there is a supportive adult to work with the student. Discuss with the adult ahead of time the behavioral and social needs of the student.

Teach the student to greet and interact with others who are a frequent part of his life. For example, all students can be taught to greet and thank people working in the lunch line, the bus driver, and their teachers.

11 Using appropriate assertiveness

> Students with ADHD may exhibit overly aggressive behavior when they try to express their needs or feelings. They need direct instruction to learn appropriate ways to be assertive.

Strategy Goal: To help the student learn how to show appropriate assertive behavior

Strategy Description: Students need to learn to distinguish between assertive and aggressive behavior. Provide concrete descriptions of each type of behavior and discuss each one. The amount or kind of descriptors will need to vary, depending on the age of the student and his ability to understand.

─Example──────

Aggressive

Speaking in a loud voice
Pushing someone out of the way or getting too close
Using angry, threatening words to express your thoughts and feelings
Interrupting another's conversation

Assertive

Speaking in a normal voice
Keeping an appropriate distance from the person you're talking to
Explaining your thoughts and feelings without getting angry
Entering a conversation at the appropriate time

Have students role-play a situation exhibiting aggressive behavior the first time, then appropriate assertive behavior the next time. Discuss the differences and how assertiveness is more effective in getting what you want while respecting others' feelings and ideas.

─Example──────

Possible situations

Needing a pencil in class—get from teacher or other student
Deciding who goes first in a kickball game
Standing in the lunch line
Handling teasing from another student

**Other Social
Skills Strategies:**

Many videotapes are commercially available on aggressive and assertive behavior. Show your students age-appropriate videos. Together brainstorm a list of things they see in the videos that indicate aggressive behavior. Have them also brainstorm a list of assertive behaviors. Compare lists and discuss how the degrees of reactions differ between the two types of behavior.

When a student acts overly aggressive, give him a second chance in handling the situation more appropriately. Discuss what was aggressive about his behavior, like his tone of voice, being too physical, or demanding too much. Then let him rehearse how to handle the situation appropriately. If possible, let him apply what he's learned by interacting with the original person again.

 ## 12 Controlling voice volume

> Students with ADHD may not recognize how loud they become when they're excited or in a situation that is overstimulating or frustrating. They need to be taught what volume levels are appropriate in various situations.

Strategy Goal:

To help the student learn to adjust his voice's "volume control" to various situations

Strategy Description:

Play a volume control game with the student to teach the concept. Create several short scripts of typical school situations, like two students working together at their seats, a student in the library, a couple of students in the lunchroom, and students on the playground. Then audiotape the situations using student volunteers.

Have the student listen to the scripts at various volume levels and indicate which one is more appropriate in each situation. For example, depending on your school rules, it may be fine for a student's voice volume to be louder in the lunchroom.

┌─Example─────────────────────

Working Together (using low voice and staying on task)

Ben: How many lines do we have to have in our scene?
Will: Mr. Fox said at least 25 altogether.
Ben: How do you want to do this?
Will: Well, let's think about it a little and then try to write a few lines.
          We might need to act them out to see if they work.
Ben: Okay, let's decide what it will be about.

Working Together (using loud voice and interrupting others)

Ben: How many lines do we have to have in our scene?
Will: Mr. Fox said it had to have at least 25.
Ben: That's bogus! We'll never get done!
Will: C'mon, Ben, let's get started and see how far we get.
Ben: Hey, James, where are you going for lunch? This assignment
          sucks, doesn't it?
Will: C'mon, Mr. Fox will get mad if we don't get going.

Other Social Skills Strategies:

Develop a subtle signal to the student when his voice becomes too loud. Perhaps a hand gesture like lowering the volume on the radio or just saying the words "volume control" may work to remind the student.

Remind a student what volume level is needed before he enters a situation. This prepares him for the transition to the activity or situation as well as allows him to try to manage his own voice behavior.

Use the audiotapes (described under the Strategy Description on the previous page) to talk about what physical actions are appropriate during each situation in addition to voice volume control. For example, it's okay to yell and run around and touch other students as part of a game of tag on the playground. On the other hand, even though students might be able to talk louder in the lunchroom, they still need to stay seated and respect each other's personal space.

> The student with ADHD needs clear explanations for how his behavior affects other students. He needs help understanding the social consequences of his inappropriate behavior.

Strategy Goal: To help the student with ADHD understand how his peers are affected by his inappropriate behavior

Strategy Description: Provide models and examples of appropriate behavior in a variety of situations. Discuss with the student the positive social consequences of such interaction. Then discuss what happens when the student's behavior is inappropriate.

┌─Example─────────────

Wait turn → Other students want to play or work with you.

Get impatient → You may not be chosen as a partner or to play on a team.

Raise hand to answer questions → Other students patiently listen.

Blurt out answer → Other students may tease and get angry with you.

Work quietly → You and other students get your work done.

Talk and interrupt → Other students can't get work done and may get angry at you. You might miss out on recess or have to stay after school to finish your work.

Other Social Skills Strategies: Develop a time-out area for the student when his behavior is overly disturbing to students and/or he is uncooperative. Once the student is able to verbalize and agree to the behavior that's expected of him, allow him to return.

For some activities, pair the student with another student who will be a good role model. Be sure to choose a student who won't hesitate to let the student know (in a positive way) how he should be acting.

Have a written plan of action designed ahead of time for any student with serious behavioral problems. You may want to meet with the student's parents, guidance counselor, principal, and regular teachers to develop such a plan. Both positive incentives for good behavior and consequences for inappropriate behavior need to be clarified in the plan. Be sure the focus is on helping the student develop appropriate social skills rather than on punishing him for not having developed them.

14 Showing respect for peers' ideas and feelings

> Students with ADHD need overt instruction in patiently listening to others express themselves and picking up on physical cues that indicate how someone else is feeling.

Strategy Goal: To provide the student with basic guidelines for showing mutual respect for peers' ideas and feelings

Strategy Description: The student with ADHD needs to be taught what's important to pay attention to and how to do it, even in social dynamics. Any time the student interacts, whether it's with the teacher or with a peer individually or in class discussion, he needs to show attention by listening and looking at the individual.

In an individual session with the student, teach him the look-and-listen technique. Role-play a conversation where it's your turn to express an idea. The student should be looking at you, listening, and cueing in to your facial expressions and body language. Have the student pay attention quietly and then paraphrase what you said and how you felt about it. Then let the student have a turn as you follow the same pattern. Role-play the situation enough times for the student to understand how to act attentively. Also discuss how good it feels to be paid attention to and have someone show respect by listening.

Later, when the student needs reminding, you can quietly say, "Look and listen, please" or point to your eyes and ears as a cue.

**Other Social
Skills Strategies:**   Have the student watch age-appropriate videotapes that teach social skills like interpreting body language, gestures, and facial expressions. Follow up with practice exercises related to the video.

Classroom rules not only ensure order in the classroom, but also act as guidelines for an environment of mutual respect. Create a large poster describing your classroom rules. Be sure they're short and easy to remember.

─Example─────────

Classroom Rules

1. Raise your hand.
2. Listen quietly and respectfully.
3. Don't put down others' ideas.
4. Respect everyone's property.

15 Controlling topic perseveration

> Students with ADHD may perseverate on a topic and annoy or distract other students in the process. They need help picking up cues that they need to switch to a new topic or let someone else talk.

Strategy Goal: To help the student pick up cues and develop a sense of timing so he does not perseverate on a topic

Strategy Description: Use humor to handle the situation without drawing unnecessary attention to the student. For example, like a game show host you might say, "Okay, Player Number 1, we've heard from you. Now let's hear from Player Number 2" to get the student to stop talking and allow someone else to talk. Develop the strategy as a routine in your classroom for all students.

If humor doesn't work, be direct and tell the student it's time for someone else to talk. The student may try to debate with you or continue to perseverate on the topic. Repeat your direction, like "Jeremy, you've had your turn to talk. Now someone else will have a turn." Ignore the student and turn your attention to the next student.

Other Social Skills Strategies:

A student may perseverate on a topic because he's anxious about it. Ask the student what else he needs to know or say about the topic. Alleviate his fears by giving him the facts or preparing him for any changes associated with the topic. If the student's perseveration is a long-standing habit that interferes too often with classroom discussions and activities, you may need to give the student an alternative activity while discussion is taking place. For example, the student may be allowed to work on the computer quietly in the back of the room. Provide the alternative activities until the student develops appropriate classroom discussion behavior. Eventually, the student may be able to choose between the alternative and participating in discussion, so he doesn't feel like he's being punished.

Seat the student in the room so he's near you during class discussions. Then by a look, subtle signal, or a quiet reminder, the student can pick up cues that help him know when to change the topic.

Chapter 7: Memory Skills

Unfortunately, one of the most serious effects of attention deficit hyperactivity disorder (ADHD) is weak memory skills. Because of a short attention span, the student is often unable to sustain concentration and keep focus long enough so she can learn and remember things. Consequently, the student's weak memory also affects her social skills, daily routines, and academic success.

It is very important, then, to provide the student with ADHD a variety of techniques for boosting memory skills and to purposely instruct her in ways that strengthen and use her memory.

The tips and strategies in this chapter will help your students with ADHD learn how to remember more effectively. Memory areas covered are listed below.

1. identifying the role of learning style
2. creating associations
3. practicing note-taking
4. chunking information
5. practicing concentration
6. classifying and categorizing
7. paraphrasing
8. providing external prompts and cues
9. allowing self-talk and subvocalization
10. using mnemonics
11. teaching with graphic organizers

Identifying the role of learning style

> Students with ADHD need to be taught with instructional techniques that meet their strongest learning styles for them to remember best.

Strategy Goal: To identify students' learning styles so instructional techniques can be adapted to fit their needs

Strategy Description: Observe your student's learning behavior over a period of time. If possible, observe the student in a variety of situations, like a math class, a language arts class, an art class, and PE. As you observe the student, make comments about the following areas.

1. What activities does the student seem to enjoy?

2. What kinds of activities seem difficult for the student?

3. When does the student seem to be paying attention and involved most? For example, is she most attentive during note-taking, participating in discussion, watching films, drawing, or conducting lab experiments?

4. What kinds of directions are provided to the student?

5. Does the student need directions repeated? In what circumstances?

Also ask the student's other teachers to carry out similar observations. Your school psychologist, guidance counselor, or special education consultant may help observe the student in classes. Compile the information and draw conclusions about the student's strongest learning style(s) and areas that need to be strengthened.

Note: Many commercial learning style inventories are available. For your junior high and high school students, it may be beneficial to have students take such an inventory.

Use the information from the observations and/or learning style inventory to create accommodations for students with ADHD. For example, if a learning style inventory indicates that a student's strongest learning style is auditory, the student should have things read aloud or provided on audiotape. Directions will also need to be spoken in addition to being written on a chalkboard or overhead.

Other Instructional Strategies:

Each time you provide directions or instruction, make sure to give them using at least two sensory modalities. For example, if you're teaching students to capitalize at the beginning of a sentence, you can write a capital letter ("big" letter) on the board at the start of a sentence. Then have students trace the capital in the air to add another modality (kinesthetic) for learning.

For strong visual learners, put labels on things so they can learn names. For example, if a student is learning the names of the nine planets, make sure each planet's name is prominently placed on the planet so students can make a name association with the planet's size and other distinguishing characteristics.

Visual learners respond well to diagrams, tables, outlines, pictures, cartoons, charts, and graphs. When preparing worksheets, notes, or activities as part of instruction, include visual material along with the written.

Some students learn better with the sense of touch or tactile modality. Have these students write out what they're learning or draw or act it out to internalize what they're learning.

◆2 Creating associations

> Students with ADHD remember best when they can relate to ideas personally. They need instruction that helps them associate new information with familiar experiences and ideas.

Strategy Goal: To provide ways for the student to associate new learning with familiar information

Strategy Description: Trying to relate to students personally can certainly keep you busy. Relating to students means:

- listening to what they talk about and do
- reading what they're reading
- watching what they're watching
- listening to what they're listening to

By learning about the students, you'll be better able to give them something to associate new information with so they can remember. You can also remind them of early concepts they've learned to help them attach meaning to newer, more complex concepts.

Anything you think students can relate to is fair game for an association.

- personal or familiar experiences
- popular cultural items like cartoon characters, songs, TV shows, toys, and cars
- familiar visual or sensory images

When you explain things, say things like the following during instruction to make associations.

—Example—

"This shape is a sphere. It's just like the ball we use to play kickball at recess."

"Amoebas have no certain shape. Just look at Bob the Blob here."

"See these holes in SpongeBob SquarePants' body? He and his other sponge relatives have holes to let in water and food. He belongs to the Porifera family (pores, get it?)."

Other Association Strategies:

When reviewing new information, have students imagine they were teaching the concepts to younger students. What familiar things or experiences would they relate to the ideas to make them clear? Have students work in pairs to brainstorm. Then let them share with the class. For example, how would they explain concepts like evaporation, hypothermia, or how a bill is ratified to a younger student? Reviewing processes are often good candidates for coming up with familiar associations.

Commercials often use visual, sound, cultural, and common experience associations to make their point. Have students remember favorite commercials. Discuss what makes each one memorable. Use familiar commercials when it seems appropriate as an associative device for remembering new ideas.

◆ 3 Practicing note-taking

> Students with ADHD often have difficulty determining what's important to remember in class content. They need instruction in how to recognize key words, phrases, and main points in what they're learning.

Strategy Goal: To help the student learn strategies for note-taking that help identify important information to know and remember

Strategy Description: For each class a student takes, she needs to learn specific strategies for recording and remembering information related to the subject matter. For example, for math class, she could write rules for certain processes and examples of math problem solutions to help illustrate them.

For a social studies class, the student will need to know country or state locations, dates and specific events, famous historical figures, and their contributions to history. The student can be taught to put this information in simple two-column charts for ease of memorization (e.g., date/event or person/contribution for column headings).

Have the student keep an individual notebook for each class in which to record notes for studying. Arrange with the teacher for extra credit points for note-taking. The note-taking and extra credit points can help balance out weaker test and quiz scores students with ADHD often get.

Other Note-taking Strategies: Have teachers provide note copies to students to follow along with as they discuss information. As the student listens, she can use a highlight marker to emphasize key points to remember. Later she can recopy the notes, but she only needs to record the most important key points for easier remembering.

When the student is presented with new material from a textbook, have her preview the material and anticipate the key information she'll be required to know. If possible, get reading assignments ahead of time so you can preview the material with the student before it is actually assigned.

Remind the student how textbooks organize and present material with titles, headings, and bold-faced words to suggest what will be important to know.

 4 ## Chunking information

> Students with ADHD often have difficulty identifying and remembering key information in what they learn. They need to develop strategies to retain key chunks of information in their memory.

Strategy Goal:

To help the student learn how to "chunk" or pare down information to make it easier to remember and retrieve when needed

Strategy Description:

Chunking is a memory strategy that involves remembering a select few details that trigger the memory of other relevant information. Chunking pares down the amount of information a student must hold on to. The chunks are the general or main ideas that prompt the recall of specific details.

Use chunking as a daily introductory review activity. On a chalkboard or overhead projector, place two or three chunks of information. Either by discussion or having students journal, have them tell what other information they recall from the "chunks" you give them. You might present sample chunks like the following.

— Example —

For a story:	key characters	conflicts
For History:	Amendment 19	Women
For Science:	stalactite—top	stalagmite—bottom
For Math:	◯	πr^2

Other Chunking Strategies:

Encourage students to use chunking cues when they begin a test or quiz. Beforehand, have them memorize as many key information chunks as they can. Allow them to write the chunks on the top of their test or answer sheets before taking tests to trigger memory. You might also allow students to use chunked notes to help answer any essay or short answer questions.

Think of practical ways for students to use chunking. For example, if a student has PE the next day and is starting a swimming unit, and also has a field trip in the afternoon, he has at least two important things to remember. The chunks that trigger his memory might be "swimming trunks" and "bus money." As a role model, frequently put your own chunks on the chalkboard to remind yourself of what to do too!

─── Example ───

birthday card

haircut

groceries

There are many chunking methods students can use. For example, show students how underlining and outlining are actually chunking note techniques. Present notes to students in outline form when first introducing information and let them fill in the gaps as they listen and learn. Later, as review, you might put up the same outline and have them orally expand on the key ideas. Word webs and maps are other excellent graphic chunking techniques.

5 Practicing concentration

> Students with ADHD need to build their concentration skills in order to remember better. They need instruction and practice to strengthen concentration.

Strategy Goal:

To help students strengthen their powers of concentration

Strategy Description:

Create concentration games and activities as part of your instruction. For example, to review concepts, let pairs of students make concentration games. Students can make flash cards to review key terms and vocabulary by putting the term on one card and its definition on another card. Have students make no more than ten term-definition sets at a time. Then each student pair can practice seeing who can match all ten terms with the correct definitions. Pairs must keep practicing until both of them have all ten correct. As students make matches, they must pronounce each word and say its definition as another way of strengthening memory.

Students can create other concentration games as active ways to review for quizzes and tests.

Other Concentration Strategies:

On an overhead projector, make things like diagrams, lists, charts, or key terms you want students to remember. Tell them to concentrate on the information for a specified time period (e.g., five minutes) and have them think to themselves of ways they can associate ideas and remember the information. Tell them you'll be shutting the overhead projector off and then asking them to write down the information from memory. You may want to start with short amounts of information or allow students to work in pairs. Increase the information and independence as students concentrate better. Use the technique regularly to help students create and master individual memory strategies.

Have fun with concentration activities. Play songs for students and see if they can remember lyrics. Use board games and interactive computer video games as other fun ways to build concentration. Many games require that students concentrate and remember in order to win a game.

6 Classifying and categorizing

> Students with ADHD may not see the connections between ideas that would help them remember them. They need instructional approaches like classifying and categorizing to help them make associations and connections.

Strategy Goal:

To provide the student with ways to connect and remember ideas through classifying and categorizing

Strategy Description:

Connecting ideas and concepts means learning through activities like grouping, classifying, categorizing, and sorting. Using manipulatives is a great hands-on way for students to classify and categorize.

Create manipulatives like cards that students can use to classify, categorize, sort, and group. Activities like the following can be used over and over in different ways depending on the concepts and information you want students to learn.

──Example──

- Have students cut out magazine pictures that are related to a specific idea or concept they are learning.

- Students in a math class could group pictures according to the target concept. Directions might say, "Make a pile of things that are round or sphere-like" to teach the geometric shape *sphere*, or "Group things together that have area and group other things that have perimeter" to distinguish those concepts.

- In a reading class, young students could cut out pictures of "things that start with **g**" or be given cards with items pictured and then sort them by beginning sounds.

- For a science class, provide students with cards that include drawings or pictures of living things. Then students might group according to categories like birds, reptiles, insects, and so on. In pairs, students could discuss features to help them classify pictures together.

Other Classifying and Categorizing Strategies:

Use graphic organizers like charts and Venn diagrams to enhance memory through classifying and categorizing. Graphic organizers can have students classify by doing things like comparing, contrasting, and listing features. Providing students with notes in chart form when presenting material, for example, gives them a visual and language hook for remembering. Or having them complete Venn diagrams over something just taught makes them think more and make more comparisons and contrasts, thus strengthening memory.

Use directions on worksheets that help students categorize, classify, and remember through connections. For example, directions for a worksheet on parts of speech to identify verbs might read like this:

"Verbs are words that end with **-ing** and **-ed**. Circle the words in the reading passage below that are verbs."

In this case, students are expected to find and classify words based on a language or word feature.

7 Paraphrasing

Some students with ADHD may not remember information because of language difficulties. They need strategies to strengthen their understanding and use of language.

Strategy Goal:

To improve the student's paraphrasing skills so she can "own," internalize, and remember information

Strategy Description:

Paraphrasing is a skill in which the student learns new ideas and concepts and then restates them in her own language for better understanding. A student remembers information best when she truly understands it.

Practice paraphrasing often as a learning activity. For example, have students look up definitions in a glossary or dictionary for their language arts, science, or history classes. Then have students write the definitions using their own words. Pairing students for the paraphrasing part of the activity works well as they have to discuss and agree upon the paraphrased definition, thus increasing time and involvement with the concepts and, hopefully, understanding.

Word	Dictionary Definition	Meaning in Your Words
emancipation	releasing from restraint, control, or power of another	freedom
amendment	legal addition to the constitution	a law that changes the constitution
civil war	war between people in the same territory	fighting among ourselves in the same country

Other Paraphrasing Strategies:

Use paraphrasing frequently to check students' understanding of assignment or activity directions. When you give directions, have two or more students paraphrase them out loud. If they understand the directions, they should be able to repeat them in their own words.

Summarizing is a form of extended paraphrasing. Have students summarize their learning instead of doing worksheets or assignments. For example, partway through a story, have them summarize the plot, conflict, and characters. Or, after a film for History or Science class, have students write a paragraph or so describing its main ideas. It's often surprising to see what students actually learn that may not be an "answer" requested on a worksheet, yet is important information.

Providing external prompts and cues

> Students with ADHD may not have instant recall of information. They need external prompts, cues, and reminders to trigger their memory.

Strategy Goal: To teach the student how to observe and use external cues to help her memory

Strategy Description: External cues or reminders can be used for a variety of things students need to remember. They can range from cues for remembering appropriate behaviors to reminders about steps to academic concepts and processes.

Whether you use a visual, auditory, or mnemonic reminder, follow these tips.

- Make eye contact before cueing.
- Use brief, concise language.
- Use the same terms, language, and short explanations for the same situation or concept each time.
- Use visual signals and gestures.

Social Cues and Reminders

Your reminder or cue for students who habitually blurt out and interrupt discussions or conversations may include a poster with the following information to help them recognize pauses in conversation.

> **Conversation and Discussion Reminders**
>
> Stop.
>
> Listen.
>
> Ask yourself, "Has the other person stopped talking?"
>
> If so, it's your turn to talk.
>
> If not, wait for the other person to stop talking.

Academic Cues and Reminders

Reminders to trigger recall of academic information can take many forms. You can use things like the following.

- posters with steps of things like math processes placed in several easy-to-see spots in the room and/or individual copies to place on desks

- pictures and colors to highlight what to remember, like having maps posted with continents outlined in blue and states/provinces within continents outlined in red so students can remember the difference

- auditory cues, like "It starts with **p**" to remind students how plants get food or "Their first letters spell HOMES" to cue students on the names of the Great Lakes.

Other Cueing Strategies:

Frequently post visual reminders for the student (e.g., rules to follow, the steps to processes, schedules, written lists of materials or directions) especially when the student must remember more than one or two items.

Put the day's agenda or plan on the same side of the chalkboard each day. If the agenda includes something new for the day (which most days it does!), prepare your ADHD students for the change. Describe what's different in terms of what they need to know that day (e.g., a test or guest speaker) or what behavior is expected.

9 Allowing self-talk and subvocalization

> Some students with ADHD are highly verbal. They benefit from strategies that allow them to talk through information to remember it.

Strategy Goal:

To provide activities that allow a student to talk while she's learning in order to strengthen memory abilities

Strategy Description:

If you notice a student who whispers or mutters to herself while working or who talks through something with you to understand it, you have a good candidate for activities involving verbalization. Any activity that allows "self-talk," whispering to oneself, and just plain talking is helpful. Activities that combine talking and writing or talking and doing also help the highly verbal student to learn.

Any classroom activity ordinarily conducted as paper-pencil has the potential to become more verbally-oriented. Use the following tips to help modify instructional activities.

Tips

- Allow the student to sit in an area where she won't bother anyone but can still talk to herself or with a partner while she's working.

- If a student is assigned to read quietly, allow her to go to a quiet place to read aloud to herself without bothering others. Or pairs of students can take turns reading to each other.

- Provide a tape recorder for the student to talk into while learning new concepts or trying to remember new ideas. Let the student record and then listen to herself to help memory. Have the student record information over and over until she knows it.

- Pair students to work together and talk through processes when they're first learning them. For example, as students work math problems, let them talk through each step aloud as it's solved. When learning how to borrow for subtraction, students might say, "I need to borrow 1 from here and carry it over to the next column. I have to make sure I cross out the number I borrowed from and lower it one number."

Other Verbal Strategies:

Allow for oral testing of students with strong verbal learning styles. These students often have better auditory memory. When they talk through information as they're testing, it often helps them remember other associated information.

Have students recite processes step-by-step aloud after you say them. Draw a picture to go with each step, but don't include the words. When you hold up a step of the process, students should describe aloud what it is. For example, if students are learning about photosynthesis in plants, put each part of the formula on a card for students to explain its connection to the making of energy.

Encourage students with strong verbal skills to develop questioning techniques to check their understanding. Frequently hold quick conferences with the student to check what she's understanding. Have her paraphrase back to you what she knows.

When giving directions, have the more verbal student repeat back to you what she understands the directions to be. This way, she hears them again by repeating them herself and you know she understands them.

10 Using mnemonics

Some students need nontraditional ways to get their attention
while learning and then to remember things. They need memory
strategies that appeal to all of their senses.

Strategy Goal: To provide the student with a variety of mnemonic or multi-
sensory memory strategies

Strategy Description: Whenever possible, use a variety of mnemonics to enhance
memory. Mnemonics include things like acronyms, acrostics
(memory sentences), rhymes, songs, and riddles. Whatever
mnemonic you create, exaggerate the information by using
silly, wild words, sounds, or ideas, or in some way relate it
to the student's personal experience and sense of humor.

Examples of Acrostics

Classification of Living Things
Kingdom
Phylum
Class
Order
Family
Genus
Species
Acrostic: **Kings Play Chess On Fine
Grains of Sand**

The Five Kingdoms of Life
(in order of most complex to least complex)
Animals
Plants
Fungi
Monerans
Protists
Acrostic: **Apes Poke Fun at Many People**

Examples of Acronyms

FACE for the four spaces on the treble clef
ROY G. BIV for the colors of the rainbow (red, orange, yellow, green,
blue, indigo, violet)
SPRAP for the five freedoms in the Bill of Rights (Speech, Press, Religion,
Assembly, Petition)

**Other Mnemonic
Strategies:** Use commercially-prepared materials that include songs,
rhymes, and riddles whenever possible to teach and review
concepts. Even "big" kids love things like "Conjunction
Junction" (*Schoolhouse Rock!—Grammar Rock* available in

audiotape from Disney) because of the rhyming and song when they have to remember parts of speech.

Have students make up rhymes and raps to memorize information. Let them share with the class by presenting live or by audiotaping or videotaping what they create.

During instruction, frequently create vivid imagery and pictures to go with new concepts. To teach about adjectives, you might use the following imagery.

Students can make up their own images or use magazine pictures to represent images they think of as they review material.

Teaching with graphic organizers

Many students with ADHD have strong visual and associative memories. These students need material presented to them in easy-to-remember and easy-to-visualize ways.

Strategy Goal: To help the student learn and remember ideas by presenting them graphically

Strategy Description: Use graphic organizers regularly as part of instruction. Have students fill in graphic organizers on worksheets and as part of note-taking. Be sure to use graphic organizers appropriate to their topics. For example, use a Venn diagram when you want to compare and contrast concepts, a chart for memorizing dates and events or people and contributions, and a flowchart for processes.

Comparing Story Characters
(*Tikki Tikki Tembo*, a Chinese folktale)

Sam	Both	Tikki Tikki Tembo
short name	brothers	long name
was saved	fell into well	died

Lysogenic Cycle

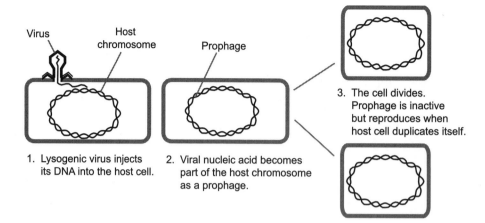

Virus Host chromosome Prophage

1. Lysogenic virus injects its DNA into the host cell.

2. Viral nucleic acid becomes part of the host chromosome as a prophage.

3. The cell divides. Prophage is inactive but reproduces when host cell duplicates itself.

Other Graphic Strategies:

When testing students over new information, use graphic organizers as part of their tests to facilitate their recall. For example, if a question on a test is to explain a scientific process, have the student fill in a blank graphic organizer similar to the one used for instruction.

When giving students class assignments or projects, have them create their own graphic organizers for the information. Provide them with examples of graphic organizers they might use (e.g., word webs, Venn diagrams, flowcharts). Then in pairs, let students think over the material and select appropriate graphic organizers. When students are finished, have them share their graphic organizers with the class either by presenting them to the class as a whole or by presenting to other pairs.

Chapter 8: Work Completion Skills

"He never finishes anything! It takes him forever to get to work! His assignments are always late! He can't sit still to work! What does it take to get his work done?"

These are typical comments from a teacher about the student with attention deficit hyperactivity disorder (ADHD).

Work completion is a very complex process. It involves getting started and staying on-task for a sustained period of time. That takes incredible self-control and self-discipline for the student with attention deficit, in particular.

Anywhere along the way, a student's lack of focus can interfere with the work completion process. However, by making accommodations within the classroom to enhance focus and train the student how to work independently, the student with ADHD can succeed.

Work completion areas covered in this chapter are listed below.

1. developing independent work habits

2. handling perfectionism and procrastination

3. making materials readily accessible

4. helping the student adjust to classroom transitions by providing predictable classroom routines and schedules

5. monitoring assignment completion daily or weekly

6. giving concise written and verbal directions

7. building a manageable level of frustration tolerance

8. learning and following classroom guidelines and expectations for work

9. designing assignments appropriate to abilities, interest level, and level of concentration

10. creating a working environment that eliminates visual and auditory distraction

11. setting up a daily schedule that facilitates and enhances the student's concentration

12. helping the student develop inner controls that keep him attentive and on-task

13. providing accommodations for writing and handwriting difficulties

14. learning how to produce quality work

15. planning and completing lengthy projects and assignments

1   Developing independent work habits

Sometimes getting started on work is the biggest hurdle for students with ADHD. They may need very structured situations to develop the habit of working independently.

Strategy Goal: To help the student learn the steps to follow in developing independent work habits

Strategy Description: Provide the student's teachers with a work log to monitor the student's progress in working independently. Each teacher can review and discuss the log with the student at the end of the class period. Later the student's core teacher or special education teacher can review the log with the student. Work logs may also be sent home if parents wish to support or reward the student's efforts.

For example, if the student had five different classes in a day, he would have five different slips at the end of the day like the following.

Class Work Log

Started working right away: Yes   No

Length of time worked:

Amount of work completed:

Comments:

Other Work Completion Strategies: Some students may benefit from the use of a kitchen timer. The timer can be set for a length of time the student must work. During that time, the student may not interrupt the teacher or other students; he must be working independently. At the end of the time, the student may take a prearranged mini-break and then return for another timed work session.

For a very young student who sits in the same desk all day, you may want to tape a work log to his desk that covers all his classes. When the student begins work, you can immediately circle "Yes" for "Started working right away" and even note the time. When the student finishes, he can raise his hand for you to return to his desk to record how long he worked and to add any other comments.

2   Handling perfectionism and procrastination

> Students with ADHD may have trouble verbalizing the status of a given assignment. Teachers may assume it has been lost, only partially done, or is being ignored altogether. A student may actually be holding onto the assignment out of fear it doesn't measure up. These students need help dealing with their perfectionism and procrastination.

Strategy Goal:

To help the student judge when an assignment meets the criteria for being handed in

Strategy Description:

For some students, rather than turn in a paper with weak handwriting, misspellings, or work partially done, it's more face-saving to turn in no assignment at all. Make sure the student understands what quality of assignment you'll accept and what each one of his teachers will accept. The student may need "coaching" for a period of time from each teacher to make sure the assignment measures up.

Make sure any assignment accommodations have already been arranged with teachers. Ensure the student understands the accommodations he's allowed. For example, he may be penalized less for spelling as long as he completes an essay writing assignment. Or, he may be allowed to turn in a math assignment with just the answers and without showing work due to handwriting difficulties that would slow down his ability to complete the assignment.

**Other Work
Completion Strategies:**

Ask the student to turn in what he has completed at the end of the work period whether he's totally finished or not. Provide positive feedback to the student for his efforts and any redirection, if needed. If the student needs more time to finish the assignment, indicate when it is to be handed in.

Provide the student with a work buddy who can help him meet the assignment criteria. That student may also need to know about any accommodations. When both students are finished with their assignments during the work period, one of the buddies takes responsibility for turning the work in.

 3 Making materials readily accessible

Many times students with ADHD misplace or forget their materials. Consequently, they spend work time searching for them and getting behind in work. These students need to be supported in developing their organizational problems and not be penalized for them.

Strategy Goal:

To provide a predictable routine for the student to follow in getting materials so he can get right to work

Strategy Description:

Depending on the severity of the student's organizational problem, work out an arrangement in each classroom for having materials readily available to him. For example, a student may be very good at remembering his notebook and book, but often forgets a pencil. Provide a spot where this student can get a pencil when he needs it without disrupting the class. You can provide the pencils or have the student purchase a package before school starts that are just for his use.

**Other Work
Completion Strategies:**

Arrange for the student to leave the previous class two or three minutes early to go to his locker to get the appropriate materials. Develop a system where the student gets any homework assignment before he leaves. With the extra time, he can arrive at the next class on time, less stressed, and ready to work.

List the materials for the next day on a consistent side of the chalkboard. Train your student to look there and jot down what he'll need for the next day so he can come prepared.

As an extra incentive, reward the student with extra credit points or an extra privilege when he comes completely prepared and gets right to work.

 4   ## Helping the student adjust to classroom transitions by providing predictable classroom routines and schedules

> Frequent transitions within a class period can interfere with a student's ability to concentrate and complete work. The student with ADHD needs predictable classroom routines and schedules to get in the habit of doing work.

Strategy Goal: To help the student adjust to predictable classroom transitions

Strategy Description: Encourage teachers to develop a somewhat predictable routine within their classrooms so students know when transitions will occur and can adjust their attention accordingly. The schedule doesn't have to be a semester or year-long routine, but one that works for a particular unit and is followed for some length of time.

─Example─

Writing Unit Classroom Routine
1. Correct Daily Oral Language sentences.
2. Read background information and examples in writing book.
3. Work on assignment.

Other Work Completion Strategies: If major classroom routines will change, make sure the student knows well ahead of time. For example, having a substitute teacher when a big assignment is due can be very upsetting to a student with ADHD.

Signal the student when a transition to a different activity is coming during the class period. Talk with the student about what to do if his assignment isn't finished before moving on. Reassuring the student and helping him problem solve the handling of incomplete work allows him to focus more calmly on what's happening next.

5 Monitoring assignment completion daily or weekly

> Students with ADHD often don't recognize the importance of completing assignments or the consequences that result when they don't. Many need daily or weekly monitoring systems to help them take conscious responsibility for improving assignment completion.

Strategy Goal: To provide a daily or weekly monitoring system to improve the student's rate of assignment completion

Strategy Description: Develop an assignment completion monitoring sheet to raise the student's awareness about what he's accomplishing. Younger students can have their progress monitored daily or, in tougher cases, have their morning and afternoon classes monitored separately. Use consequences and incentives based on the results.

Older students, or those with less severe assignment completion problems, can take a slip around to their teachers on Fridays (I often get them to start taking it around on Thursday so there are no excuses for getting responses from all teachers by Friday). You might also add a spot for a parent signature. Sample forms are provided for your use on page 113. Be sure to make a copy of the completed form for your own records before sending a copy home for parents to read and sign.

Daily Progress Form

Name _____

Date _____

Class	Teacher	Were all assignments completed?		Comments
_____	_____	Yes	No	_____
_____	_____	Yes	No	_____
_____	_____	Yes	No	_____
_____	_____	Yes	No	_____
_____	_____	Yes	No	_____

Weekly Progress Form

Student _____

Week Ending _____

Class	Number of Assignments	Number Completed	Grade

_____   _____
Resource Teacher Signature   Parent Signature

**Other Work
Completion Strategies:**
Design a reward or point system to use with the assignment completion forms. For example, a student could earn five minutes extra recess if he completes all morning assignments. Or an older student who reaches an agreed upon goal on his assignment completion sheet can earn a trip to the school snack bar instead of sitting in study hall. You might also want to work out a reward system with parents. For example, 80% assignment completion for the week means the student can go to the movies with a friend or have driving privileges.

6 Giving concise written and verbal directions

Students with ADHD may have difficulty completing assignments because they don't understand the directions. They need a combination of concise written and verbal directions to know what to do.

Strategy Goal:
To provide a predictable direction-giving routine that ensures a student receives directions he can understand and follow

Strategy Description:
Make it a habit to provide directions for assignments both in written and verbal form. Give the student written directions via a short list on the chalkboard or a slip of paper he can keep in front of him. Have the student listen while you verbally explain the written directions. You might even write out the directions like a short checklist the student can use to make sure he covers each step of the assignment.

If you don't want to use separate slips of paper, have the student copy the directions at the top of the paper he'll be using for the assignment. He can still use it as a checklist.

☐ Read pages 1-8 in your novel.

☐ On a separate sheet of paper, write a summary of what you read.

☐ Put the summary in your reading folder.

**Other Work
Completion Strategies:**

Before giving any kind of directions, use an alert cue to get the student's and/or class's attention. You might say something like, "Everyone look at me and get ready to listen." As soon as everyone is attentive, provide verbal and written directions.

Individually check in with students who have problems with attention to see if they understand the directions. With a highlight marker, highlight the key words in worksheet directions so students can focus in on what to do.

 7 **Building a manageable level of frustration tolerance**

Because the student with ADHD has trouble knowing how much to pay attention and what to focus on, he can become easily frustrated. The student needs help building his frustration tolerance to a manageable level by regulating how much information is directed at him and how fast.

Strategy Goal:

To help the student increase his ability to retain information or directions and complete a chunk of work appropriate to his needs

Strategy Description:

Many times in a classroom, students are given three activities to complete within a class period with all the directions provided at once or, in some cases, provided midway through completion of the prior activity. The student with ADHD gets totally frustrated at this kind of pace and pressure.

Give the student only one set of directions and one activity to do at a time. Provide written directions for the student to refer to. When he finishes the activity, he can get the next set of directions and continue on. Make sure the student knows about how long to devote to each activity. You might write the time to end work or to allot for the activity on the direction sheet itself.

Other Work Completion Strategies:

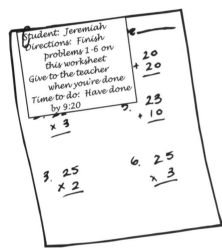

As long as the student remains on task, allow him to work at his own pace. When he completes the task, he can go to the teacher for the next worksheet or activity directions.

Provide the student with a method for time out when he becomes frustrated and overwhelmed. He might say, "I need to get a drink of water" as his signal to you that he needs a short break and will then get right back to work. Make sure the student checks in when he returns from the drinking fountain and gets any help he needs.

 8 **Learning and following classroom guidelines and expectations for work**

> Students with ADHD don't always understand what it means to be "working" in the classroom. For each class, a student with ADHD needs concrete guidelines so he can get to work and be productive in that particular classroom.

Strategy Goal:

To help the student learn and follow the guidelines and expectations for work expected in each of his classrooms

Strategy Description:

Have each of the student's teachers develop a functional daily checklist of guidelines and expectations for completing work in the classroom. Each teacher can review the list with the student and monitor the student's ability to follow it each day.

Mrs. Reilly's Reading Class (Elementary)

- ❑ 1. Enter the classroom quietly.
- ❑ 2. Get your reading folder from the bin.
- ❑ 3. Get your reading book.
- ❑ 4. Sit in your assigned seat.
- ❑ 5. Wait quietly for Mrs. Reilly to give the day's instructions.

Mr. McEwen's Keyboarding Class (Secondary)

- ❑ 1. Enter the classroom quietly.
- ❑ 2. Pick up a copy of the assignment directions from the black tray on the teacher's desk.
- ❑ 3. Sit at your assigned computer without talking.
- ❑ 4. Work on the assignment until five minutes before the end of class.
- ❑ 5. Print out your work and put it in the gray tray on the teacher's desk.

Other Work Completion Strategies:

Some students have more difficulty completing work in one classroom situation versus another. For example, a student may readily get to work in a math classroom where the expectations and guidelines are more routine, but have difficulty in a science class where work alternates between seat work or labs and experiments. For the more difficult situations or for times when the routine varies, develop a list like the examples above specific to the situation and review it with the student well ahead of time so he can easily make the transition.

Teachers may want to consider a "work" grade as an incentive for students who need to learn to be more productive. For example, a student may earn an extra two points per day for following the rules and guidelines. An additional ten points per week can have a big impact on the student's overall grade.

9 Designing assignments appropriate to abilities, interest level, and level of concentration

> The student with ADHD may be unable to do an assignment because he lacks the skills or the level of concentration required to complete it. Students with ADHD need to be given work that is appropriate, relevant, and doable.

Strategy Goal: To help the student develop the skill to select work he can do according to his abilities, interest level, and level of concentration

Strategy Description: Encourage teachers to frequently provide students, particularly students with ADHD, alternative assignments that still meet the same objective.

---Example---

Assignment Objective: To show an understanding of three-dimensional geometric figures

Assignment Choices

1. Make a poster with drawings and examples of each geometric figure.

2. Bring in everyday items that are examples of three-dimensional geometric figures.

3. Using the three-dimensional figure shapes we covered in math class, have an individual conference with the teacher. Tell the teacher the name of each figure and its characteristics.

Other Work Completion Strategies: Make sure that the materials students use are within their instructional level. For example, a weak reader may need to be given alternative reading material or worksheets to accomplish the same task.

Check frequently with classroom teachers if the student is on a 504 plan or an IEP and entitled to accommodations. Teachers often need help adjusting assignments to accommodate the needs of a student with ADHD.

10 Creating a working environment that eliminates visual and auditory distraction

> The student with ADHD can be highly distracted by visual or auditory stimuli when expected to work independently. This student needs a more individually-designed environment that enhances his ability to focus and be productive.

Strategy Goal:
To provide the student with a working environment that eliminates visual and auditory distraction

Strategy Description:
Suggest to teachers that they provide an individual "office" for the student where he can go to do independent work. The "office" might be a study carrel or a quieter, less distracting place in a corner of the room. The student should be expected to be with the class for instructional times, but then allowed to move to the office for independent seat work.

Stock the "office" with books, paper, pens, pencils, and any other items that help the student be productive. You might also include a folder for the student that includes the day's assignment so there are as few transitions and opportunities for distraction or off-task behavior as possible.

Other Work Completion Strategies:
Some students like to talk to themselves (subvocalize) while working through an assignment. Make sure the spot where the student works allows him to subvocalize and pay attention to his own work without distracting others.

For older, more independent students, one option for a work environment could be your school library. Many libraries have study carrels or small side rooms where the student can work distraction-free. Be sure to make arrangements with your library staff ahead of time.

11 **Setting up a daily schedule that facilitates and enhances the student's concentration**

> Students with ADHD have varying levels of attention throughout the school day. They work better at some times of the day than others. They need a daily class schedule that recognizes these needs and helps take advantage of the times when they are most focused and productive.

Strategy Goal:

To create a daily schedule that facilitates and enhances the student's ability to focus and get work done

Strategy Description:

Meet with or get input regarding the student's most productive times from a variety of people. Include the student's parents, the student himself, any previous teachers, and the school nurse if medications are involved. Along with the student's counselor, hand schedule classes to optimize productivity. For example, for a student who takes morning medication at school, it may be better to start with a PE class than a math class. Since math requires more intense concentration, it would be better to schedule it later (so the student's medication has time to take effect).

Other Work Completion Strategies:

If a schedule can't totally meet the student's needs, encourage teachers to use strategies within their classes to enhance the student's concentration. They may want to look at their overall lesson plan for the hour and anticipate when a student may be more attentive and productive within that period. Any activities requiring more intense concentration could occur at that time.

Be prepared to get creative and flexible with scheduling to meet students' needs. Some students may work better on certain types of activities at different times and with fewer students around. For labs or tests, for example, a student may need to complete these before or after school to be most productive and focused. Whenever possible, do any rescheduling at the teacher's convenience. (I always have chocolate on hand to send along with my notes and requests to teachers or as "thanks" for those who willingly make changes for my kids.)

12 ▸ Helping the student develop inner controls that keep him attentive and on-task

> Students with ADHD tend to have weak internal control and a poor sense of time. They may not know how long they have attended to any given task or what an appropriate amount of time (short or long) is to do something well. These students need help developing inner controls that keep them attentive and on-task.

Strategy Goal:

To help the student extend his ability to concentrate and remain on-task through external controls, and eventually through internal monitoring

Strategy Description:

With the student, determine a cue that lets him know he's off task and needs to return to the activity. A subtle hand gesture (I move my hand like I'm writing for written work) and quick eye contact can work well to cue the student without disrupting the rest of the class or making it a bigger "issue" than it needs to be. Praise the student later for good concentration.

Using proximity, that is being near the student when giving him directions or reading a passage, may help the student stay on-task.

Other Work Completion Strategies:

A student may be able to extend concentration time by taking a mini-break and then immediately returning to work. Make an additional seat available in the classroom for when the student needs to move. Have an understanding that when he moves, he is not to distract anyone, and that once he moves, he must immediately return to the task at hand. Another student may need to stand while reading in order to enhance his concentration. Carefully prepare your class for the exception in classroom rules by saying something like, "Jesse sometimes needs to stand or move to help him pay attention."

Determine what a particular student looks or acts like when he's concentrating. For example, one student might doodle on a piece of paper while listening to a story and may appear to be inattentive. In reality, the student is using the doodling to engage his overactivity, thus allowing him to concentrate better. Another student might put his head down to control the activity. Other teachers may need help understanding that the student isn't purposely defying rules or being lazy, but trying to help himself concentrate.

 13 ◆ **Providing accommodations for writing and handwriting difficulties**

Students with ADHD often have writing and legibility problems. They find it challenging and frustrating to do written assignments and need accommodations to alleviate such difficulties.

Strategy Goal: To provide the student with the means to produce written work without worrying about the quality of handwriting or writing in general

Strategy Description: Many accommodations can be made within the classroom to determine what the student knows (the real purpose of assignments) without penalizing the student or stressing him out due to weak writing and handwriting skills.

───Example───

Classroom Writing Accommodations

1. Decrease or eliminate how much copying the student has to do. If other students are not allowed to write on a worksheet or test copy, make sure this student has that privilege so that his writing and copying skills don't interfere with his ability to get his work done.

2. As long as the student listens and pays attention, provide him with copies of notes. He can highlight important concepts with a highlight marker while listening or copy the notes later at his own pace.

3. Have a computer available in the room so the student can word process his assignments. Spell checkers, grammar checkers, and being able to type an assignment enable the student to do his best work with little frustration.

Other Work Completion Strategies:

Allow the student to do his homework via tape recorder. Voice-activated tape recorders that use small cassettes are available and easy for a student to carry around. The student's teachers can use a similar tape recorder so they can listen and check the student's assignments.

Let students do assignments in pairs. Pair the student with weak writing skills with a student with stronger writing skills who can record the pair's answers.

14 Learning how to produce quality work

> Many students with ADHD hurriedly complete assignments without regard to quality. They need to learn the characteristics of and be able to produce quality work.

Strategy Goal:

To help the student develop internal quality control and be able to monitor his work quality independently before handing in assignments

Strategy Description:

When giving assignment directions, provide a short checklist of what the student needs to do to turn in quality work. The student can check boxes indicating he reviewed his work for specific characteristics before turning it in. Provide space on the checklist for the teacher to do the same, as well as space for a grade if desired.

Quality Math Assignment	Student	Teacher
Date _____		
Answers easy to read		
Directions followed		
All work shown		
Answers checked with calculator		
Grade _____		

Other Work Completion Strategies:

If a student hands in an assignment that doesn't yet meet your quality expectations, return the assignment to the student for improvement. Provide the student with written comments that redirect his efforts. If the student does the assignment over, have him attach the first attempt to the second. Show the student the difference in grade that results from a quality assignment.

Praise students often for quality work. Use stickers and stamps to put comments on papers that emphasize quality work and lots of effort.

Create a bulletin board with examples of your students' quality work. By each example, label what made the work quality, like "Jeremy showed all his work!" or "Samantha's title page is nicely designed and includes all the right information." Change the examples on the bulletin board frequently to reward quality efforts often and make quality a matter of routine.

> Time management, in general, is a problem for students with ADHD. They need help planning and completing large projects or assignments that extend over a period of time.

Strategy Goal: To provide the student with systems for chunking work and allocating appropriate amounts of time for each

Strategy Description: When a student is assigned a major written assignment or other project, set aside a conference time for planning and creating a time line for completing it. Each subsequent work day, hold a short conference with the student at the beginning of the class period to check his progress in accomplishing the goals set for that work period. Work periods can include time spent at home or with a resource teacher too. A list of needed materials may also be a helpful reminder.

Project: Research and create a model of a planet.

Materials Needed: computer disk, art and construction materials for planet

Work Day 1: Visit library and find information about the planet.
At home, write rough draft of planet report.

Work Day 2: Type up report about the planet using library information.
With resource teacher, proofread planet report.

Work Day 3: Gather materials for planet and begin to make it.

Work Day 4: Finish making planet.

Work Day 5: Share planet report and model with the class.

Other Work Completion Strategies:

Use weekly calendars on a regular basis to let students know the plan for each day of the week. This allows them to plan ahead and allocate time for completing work or studying for quizzes and tests. A weekly calendar is valuable for students who are in the process of learning to use and set up their own assignment notebooks or other systems. Printing the calendar on colored paper (e.g., blue for science), makes it easy for students to find among their other materials.

Create a reward system for students who manage to follow and meet project time lines. Some students may need a reward on a daily basis while others can be rewarded at the end of the project. Rewards can include things like gum or candy, leaving a few minutes early for lunch or recess, or playing a computer game when work is done.

Chapter 9: Mathematics

Have you ever considered what it really takes for you to solve a math problem? Imagine having attention deficit hyperactivity disorder (ADHD). How might that affect your ability to do math?

"Math" is not simply an arithmetical process. It requires fine-motor skills, visual-perceptual skills, reading comprehension skills, reasoning and problem-solving skills, and calculating skills. Math requires that a student be able to do the following.

- use long- and short-term memory to learn things like math facts and understand fractions
- align numbers, signs, and decimals correctly
- write neatly so a problem and answer can be read
- perceive dimensions in objects and diagrams
- read, interpret, and solve word problems
- organize and interpret information in charts and graphs
- make transitions between operations
- solve multi-step problems
- work quickly
- focus on detail and be perfectly accurate
- use a calculator

The strategies and activities in this chapter will help students with ADHD master math computation skills, improve reasoning skills, and improve or accommodate for the visual and fine-motor skills required to do math.

Math areas covered are:

1. using visual cues and formats to complete math processes correctly

2. using multi-modality strategies for learning and remembering math facts, strategies, and processes

3. accommodating for coordination or copying problems

4. paying attention to detail and striving for accuracy

5. learning "direction vocabulary" so directions can be followed accurately

6. reading and comprehending word problems

7. enhancing visual attention and rote memory

1 Using visual cues and formats to complete math processes correctly

> Some students with ADHD may have visual tracking problems that cause them to be inaccurate when doing math. They need math assignments structured so they can focus on the correct order or direction of steps.

Strategy Goal: To provide visual cues and formats so students complete math processes correctly

Strategy Description: If there is "directionality" in a math operation or process, provide a visual cue or format so it can be completed accurately.

To add two-digit numbers without carrying:

$$\begin{array}{r} \text{L R} \\ 62 \\ +31 \\ \hline \mathbf{93} \end{array}$$

Add the numbers on the Right (R).

Then add the numbers on the Left (L).

Make each individual student a strategy card to use at his desk while also illustrating the process on the chalkboard or overhead projector. Different colored markers could also be used to write the *L* and *R* and indicate the two separate columns.

Have students repeat the process aloud as they're using it to help their memory, and so you can check their understanding of the steps in the process.

Other Visual Tracking Strategies: When students are working with columns of numbers, like in three-digit addition, have them separate the numbers a little more than usual and then put vertical lines between each column so they add the correct numbers.

Have graph paper with large grid blocks on hand to use frequently. For some students with copying difficulties, write problems in the boxes for them when you give an assignment. Then have them follow the boxes to complete a process accurately. Graph paper is particularly helpful when students are learning two- and three-digit division and higher.

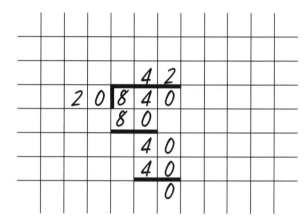

Whenever you can, use arrows for direction or use color coding with markers as you illustrate a process on the overhead transparency. Provide enough visual cues, but not so many that the process becomes over-cluttered and distracting.

When providing math problems for practice, initially give students problems that are alike and follow the same order or "directions" to complete. After students master "how" problems are done, mix up problem types for them to practice.

2   Using multi-modality strategies for learning and remembering math facts, strategies, and processes

> Students with ADHD may have difficulty remembering facts, strategies, and processes due to inconsistent levels of attention. They need multi-modality instructional strategies to learn, practice, and remember new math concepts and processes.

Strategy Goal: To provide the student with strategies for learning and remembering math facts, strategies, and processes

Strategy Description: When you present new math concepts or processes, provide instruction, practice, and reinforcement through a variety of learning modalities. Instruction is likely to take more time and creativity, but mastery and acquisition of strategies are more likely to happen.

A sample four-day lesson plan might include these components, no matter how simple or complex a process or concept may be.

Days 1 and 2: Present the concept or process using manipulatives or another hands-on method. Teach any math vocabulary or formulas associated with the new material.

Day 3: Practice on the computer using related software. Software is interactive and provides variety in format. Many programs provide instant feedback to the student.

Note: A list of web sites for locating math-related software is provided in the Resources section, page 215.

Day 4: Give students paper and pencil practice and application of facts or process.

┌─ Example ─────────────────

Sample Lesson Plan

Concept: Area of Geometric Figures

Days 1 and 2: Using purchased geometric shapes, discuss the name of each shape and what dimensions it has (e.g., sides, diameter, radius, height).

Learn the formulas for the area of each shape (e.g., cube, sphere, pyramid).

Day 3: Have students use a software program to practice finding the area of geometric figures. Allow students to work in pairs, putting a stronger math student with one who many need extra instruction.

Day 4: Create real-life word problems using geometric figures and have students solve them on paper.

**Other
Memory Strategies:**   Present new material in small chunks. Have your students create strategy cards or reminders to help them remember. Allow students to use the cards on tests, if needed.

Adding Fractions with the Same Denominator

Numerator (the number on the top)
_____
Denominator (the number on the bottom)

1. Add the numerators (top numbers).
2. Keep the denominators the same (bottom numbers).

Example:

1. Add top. $\dfrac{1}{4} + \dfrac{2}{4} = \dfrac{3}{4}$
2. Keep the same.

Once students master the process for adding fractions with like denominators, move on to subtracting fractions with like denominators. A logical third lesson would be to add fractions with like denominators that result in a "top-heavy" fraction requiring conversion to a whole number and fraction. Staying within a consistent concept or relationship, such as using same denominators, helps reinforce each process so students will remember and master it.

Make large posters of the current math process or strategy being learned. Place the same poster in several areas of the classroom as visual reminders.

Let a couple of students work together at the chalkboard. Encourage students to talk through the process as they work a problem. Hearing the process and working in a larger space often helps students learn and internalize the process.

 ## 3 Accommodating for coordination or copying problems

> Some students with ADHD have fine motor coordination or copying problems and may need extra accommodations to help keep the focus on learning math concepts.

Strategy Goal: To provide classroom accommodations for coordination or copying problems

Strategy Description: Make already prepared worksheets for the student to use in completing an assignment rather than have the student copy from a textbook and risk inaccuracy. For example, if a student is to complete problems 1-15 on page 53, word process the problems on an individual worksheet for the student.

For easier reading, type the problems. Don't handwrite them. Be sure to make the numbers large enough (computers are great for adjusting type and number size) and allow plenty of room for the student's calculation.

Other Math Strategies: Purchase consumable workbooks or prepared worksheets for students with fine motor and copying problems. These students could be given a parallel assignment in the workbook to what's being covered in class.

When doing practice problems in class before an assignment is given, let the student use a dry erase marker on white board instead of paper and pencil. This method makes it easier for the student to erase mistakes. While the rest of the class practices on paper, the student with ADHD can calculate using the white board.

4 Paying attention to detail and striving for accuracy

> Students with ADHD need direct instruction in how to be accurate when completing math processes and extra time to ensure they do so.

Strategy Goal: To provide a method for completing math assignments that helps the student pay attention to detail and strive for accuracy

Strategy Description: To encourage and build care for accuracy in assignment completion, grade the completion of the process and the steps, not just getting the right answer. Include a brief "rubric" for grading each assignment that stresses slowing down and being accurate. Leave space on the rubric for helpful comments and directions too. (See the example on page 134.)

Other Math Strategies: Pair students to check each other's work. Put a student with ADHD with a math student who is strong in accuracy and also able to explain the steps or process for solving problems. Let each student check half of their peer's assignment. For example, one student might check the odd-numbered problems, while the other student checks the even-numbered problems. Students then write their initials indicating they've checked assignments, correct any inaccurate problems, and then turn the assignments in. Keep the same student pairs so they build strong working relationships.

Once students understand and can follow steps to a process, allow them to use a calculator. Encourage them to work through a problem twice, if time allows, so they can double-check their work using a calculator.

Let students redo or correct problems for a better grade and to increase their mastery of the process or facts. For example, students may redo and "upgrade" assignments as long as they are handed in prior to a major quiz or test over the concepts.

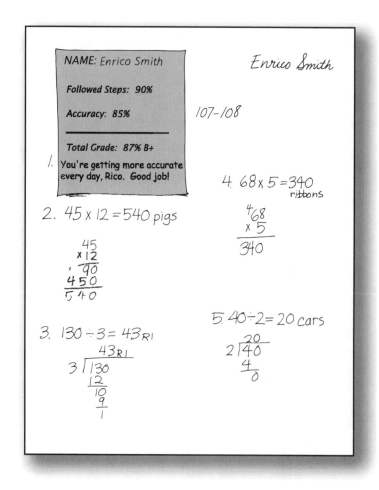

5 **Learning "direction vocabulary" so directions can be followed accurately**

> Students with ADHD may have difficulty completing math assignments because they don't understand the directions. They need direct instruction first in any "direction vocabulary" before beginning work.

Strategy Goal: To help students develop a "direction vocabulary" so they can understand and follow directions accurately

Strategy Description: Before beginning any assignment, go through the directions with your students. With a highlight marker, colored pen or pencil, or through circling, have students find words telling the operations they are to use to solve the problems. Do the same for any word problems on the page.

Provide students with a "glossary card" to keep at their desks for reference each time they do an assignment. You might laminate the glossary cards for extended use and durability.

After students find the direction words, they can then put the appropriate symbol (e.g., + , –) above the word to indicate the operations they are to use.

Direction Glossary

Words that Tell You to Subtract	Words that Tell You to Add
decrease	increase
reduce	add on to
less	more than

Adjust or add to the glossary as students learn more complex operations.

Other Direction Strategies:

For students having a lot of trouble following directions, create worksheets with as minimal directions as possible. Also group problems according to similar operations. For example, you might put two-column addition problems and then word problems using two-column addition on the same page. Vary the wording indicating the addition operation to help students learn the vocabulary, but don't mix operations like addition and subtraction on the same page.

Make directions easy to read and follow. For example, if directions are suggesting a two-step process, visually arrange the directions so students know two steps are expected. Provide a sample problem of what you expect when the steps are followed completely.

─── Example ───

Directions

1. Solve each algebra equation below.
2. Check your answers afterward. Show your work.

Example

Solve

$$2a + 10 = 32$$
$$2a + 10 - 10 = 32 - 10$$
$$2a = 22$$
$$2a \div 2 = 22 \div 2$$
$$a = 11$$

Check

$$2a + 10 = 32$$
$$2(11) + 10 = 32$$
$$22 + 10 = 32$$
$$32 = 32$$

> Because students with ADHD may have weak reading comprehension skills as well as difficulties problem-solving and reasoning, their abilities to solve word problems may be affected. They need direct instruction in solving word problems and many opportunities for guided practice before they can do word problems independently.

Strategy Goal: To teach students how to read and comprehend word problems so they make correct computational choices

Strategy Description: Provide multiple-choice computational possibilities after any word problems you assign. Have students read through the problem and choose the correct computational process. Tell them to be ready to justify their choice of computation based on the relationships explained in the problem.

---Example---

Sheena wants to play soccer this spring. She will need to buy soccer shoes ($30), a team soccer shirt ($22), soccer shorts ($25), and shin guards ($18). Sheena has saved $20 from baby-sitting. How much more does Sheena need to pay for all her soccer equipment?

a. $30
    $22
    $25
    $18
 + $20

b. $30
    $22
    $25
 + $18
    $95

    $95
 − $20
    ?

Go over students' choices as a class or individually before they actually do any problem solving or computation. Guide students through the reasoning for the correct choice by looking at the vocabulary used and relationships described between the numbers given. Then have students actually solve the word problems.

Other Word Problem Strategies:

Make up word problems based on real-life situations that occur in your classroom, school, or your students' environments. Practice word problem solving on a regular basis to get students used to the kind of reasoning involved.

---Example---

Eli has $3.00 left in his lunch account at school. Lunch costs $1.40 a day. How soon does he need to bring more money to school if he has to pay for lunch today?

$3.00		$1.60	
−1.40	(today)	−1.40	(tomorrow)
$1.60		$ .20	

Answer: tomorrow or the day after so he has it when he needs it

Put word and computational problems on the same page so students understand that math involves reading and reasoning on a regular basis as well as computation. Don't mix operations until students have mastered each type of problem or operation. Teach students a strategy to follow as they decide how to solve word problems.

---Example---

1. Read the problem.
2. Choose the numbers to use.
3. Decide what you need to find.
4. Set up the numbers.
5. Decide on the sign(s).
6. Predict the answer.
7. Solve the problem.

7   Enhancing visual attention and rote memory

> Students with ADHD need methods, steps, and processes over-exaggerated to enhance their visual attention and rote memory.

Strategy Goal: To use materials and methods that focus students' visual attention and enhance rote memory

Strategy Description: Use color coding (shaded areas in the example below) to highlight different steps in a mathematical operation. Problem examples can be done with colored chalk on a chalkboard or different colored markers on a dry erase board. Some students may even wish to use different colored markers on their own papers as they first practice operations.

---Example---

Adding Negative Numbers

-11	Both signs are ⊟.
-9	Add the two numbers.
-20	Keep the same ⊟ sign.

Adding Positive Numbers

+8	Both signs are ⊞.
+6	Add the two numbers.
+14	Keep the same ⊞ sign.

Other Visual Attention and Memory Strategies: Accompany methods for strengthening visual memory with methods that strengthen other kinds of memory. A concept might be taught using visual and kinesthetic techniques. For example, a huge number line might be drawn on a playground (or the school parking lot for the big kids!) to teach the concept of positive and negative numbers and operations involving them. Students adding -4 and -5 would physically move on the number line and realize that as they're "adding" negative numbers, they are actually making a number that has even less value than 0.

Create visual references often to refer to and manipulate when students are learning new processes and methods. Make the visuals "bigger than life" so students can't miss them.

Chapter 10: Reading and Literature

A student's ability to read and to comprehend may be affected in a variety of ways. Reading anything from literature to content area materials requires the student to focus and attend to a multitude of tasks at one time. The student must do the following:

- decode and identify words
- keep her place while reading
- attend to and identify important details
- comprehend information
- remember important details for recall later on
- take in large amounts of information at one time

If the student's focus and attention are sporadic, inconsistent, or inadequate during any of these steps or processes, her overall reading ability and, consequently, her academic performance may suffer.

The activities and strategies in this chapter are designed to strengthen students' reading skills in the following areas.

1. improving visual memory, especially related to sight word vocabulary
2. strengthening and applying word decoding skills
3. following written directions
4. accommodating reading disabilities
5. sustaining concentration to reading materials
6. locating, learning, and remembering important details in content areas
7. enhancing comprehension
8. improving listening comprehension
9. strengthening visual attention to important details
10. identifying and remembering important details in literature
11. understanding graphic material like pictures, graphs, and charts

1 ### Improving visual memory, especially related to sight word vocabulary

> Students with attention deficit hyperactivity disorder (ADHD) may have weak visual-memory skills that affect their ability to remember common sight words. They need multisensory approaches to help them learn and remember sight words.

Strategy Goal: To help the student learn and apply memory techniques for learning new sight words

Strategy Description: Let the student use a computer to type new words she needs to learn. Increase the type size to 48-point type, for example, to enhance visual memory. Have the student type each word several times. Each time the student types the word, she should pronounce it first and then spell it as she types.

when	laugh

Other Reading Strategies: Have the student create her own flash cards for new sight words. After using the typing technique above, she can cut out each word and put it on an index card. She can then use the words to test herself, or have the teacher or a reading buddy show her each card to read aloud.

Make the student's reading list also her spelling list to reinforce memory and learning. Create short sentences to dictate to the student using each word so the student has a context for usage. Have the student check over her own spelling when she's done. This would be a good time to practice punctuation and capitalization too.

—Example—

I sit on the floor when I read.

My brother makes me laugh.

Attention and focusing problems may affect the visual and auditory memory skills of students with ADHD. They need multi-modality instruction to help them use and strengthen these skills, especially in relationship to word decoding.

Strategy Goal: To provide students with a variety of multi-modality choices for acquiring decoding and other reading skills

Strategy Description: Cut colored overlays into smaller pieces so an overlay can be used to separate and analyze a part of a word. For example, with a unit on prefixes meaning "not," the overlay can be placed on the prefix so the student isolates the prefix from the main word. Make the words larger on cards or a worksheet to enhance visual attention. The student can read the words as follows.

unbelievable	not	believable
abnormal	not	normal
imperfect	not	perfect

Other Word Decoding Strategies: Record new words assigned to students on an audiotape. After each word, pause so the student can repeat the word as she listens. Have a print copy of the word for the student too. If necessary, read the word a couple of times, having the student repeat the word each time. For some students, recognition is enhanced by having them also trace an enlarged copy of the word with a pencil and sound out word parts as they trace.

Create a reading center with a computer and software programs. Software programs are great for repetitive tasks; they provide immediate feedback, and they tend to heighten attention and interest. If possible, obtain software with both visual and auditory components. Some suggestions are provided in the References section on page 216.

3 ⬥ Following written directions

> Students with ADHD need written directions presented to them in ways that are easy to understand and remember.

Strategy Goal: To provide students with clear, step-by-step directions in manageable chunks so they can successfully and accurately complete work

Strategy Description: On an individual sheet for each student, list the steps for an assignment's directions in the order you want students to complete them. Encourage students to check off each step as they finish it in order to monitor their own progress.

☑ 1. Summarize in writing what happened in the story you just read.

❑ 2. Think of a way the story could have ended differently. On the same sheet of paper, write a paragraph telling your ending.

❑ 3. Using an ink pen, copy your new ending in neat handwriting on the paper your teacher gives you.

❑ 4. Draw a picture above your paragraph that goes with your ending.

❑ 5. Place your picture and paragraph on the teacher's desk by the end of the class period.

Other Written Direction Strategies: Use the same step-by-step direction-listing strategy as above, but place each numbered direction on an individual index card or strip of paper. As a student finishes, she turns the card over. Being able to see and monitor her own progress allows the student to feel successful as she works.

Accompany your written step-by-step directions with a copy on the chalkboard or overhead. When students ask you to repeat directions, tell them to consult their individual and overhead copies rather than relying on you.

Provide students with directions in a step-by-step format every time. Develop a predictable pattern related to your subject matter that the student can follow. Being consistent with direction "language" and format helps focus the student's attention and prevents confusion when presented with new tasks.

4 Accommodating reading disabilities

Some students with ADHD may also have reading disabilities. They need additional accommodations to help them learn to read and pay attention.

Strategy Goal:

To provide the student with reading accommodations to use in the classroom and at home

Strategy Description:

Make audiotapes of material you expect your students to read. You can either make them yourself or ask older students or school volunteers to make them. Then have a listening center with tape player and earphones available where the student can listen and "mouth" or read along with the material at her own pace.

Include places where you ask the student to pause the tape and think about crucial questions, like what they think will happen next or what they think the main problem or conflict is for a character. Be sure to include answers to the questions on the audiotape. Or, at a pause, you can have the student practice reading trickier, new words you noticed in the passage. Provide the student with a word list and page references ahead of time.

Let students check out audiotapes so they can practice rereading the story at home or with a parent.

Audiotapes are also great for absent students or students who need to listen again for better comprehension.

**Other
Reading Strategies:**

Scan any reading worksheets onto a computer that has a text-to-speech program. Then let the student "read" the worksheet and write written responses to questions using word processing.

Allow students to read in pairs to accomplish an assignment. Select a reading partner who is patient and supportive for the student with the reading disability. For such partnerships, you may want to designate how much each partner reads, based on ability and need. However, each student should be expected to complete the accompanying assignment.

Locate the same reading materials, but in a high-interest, low-vocabulary format. Allow the student to use the material to complete a similar or the same assignment as her peers.

 5 Sustaining concentration to reading materials

> Students with ADHD need help sustaining concentration on reading tasks so they can understand and remember what they read.

Strategy Goal:

To structure reading tasks in a way that helps the student concentrate more effectively

Strategy Description:

Break the reading into logical sections with short activities interspersed in between to help concentration and comprehension. For example, have students draw a picture of the event just read about and write a main idea caption for it.

For older students or more sophisticated readers, pause a story along the way and have students draw pictures on a plot line of each complication faced by the main character as the plot advances.

Example

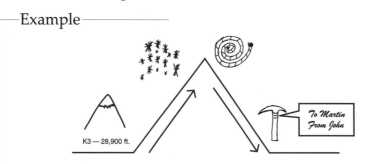

Picture Key

 Mountain. Paul Osborn (age 26) and Martin Nace (age 40+) begin to climb K3 (Kalpurthia) in the Himalayas.

 Snowflakes. It snows and the climbers have to stop.

 Climbing rope. Nace falls to his death saving Osborn. Osborn had ignored Nace's warnings about climbing.

 Ice axe. Engraved "To Martin From John." Left on the summit of K3 by Paul Osborn. Osborn doesn't take credit.

"Top Man." James Ramsey Ullman. *Elements of Literature*, Third Course. Holt, Rinehart, & Winston, Inc. Chicago: 1993.

Other
Concentration Strategies: If the reading selection is relatively short, let the student read it into an audiotape first (as long as the student doesn't have decoding problems). Then have the student listen to her reading of the selection again. At that time, provide the student with a study guide or story map to complete as she rereads.

For a student who is physically very hyperactive, let her pace back and forth in a small area of the room while reading. This strategy helps control the student's impulsivity and lets her focus on the reading task.

6 Locating, learning, and remembering important details in content areas

> Students with ADHD need help focusing on what's important to know and remember in their content area reading assignments. Without specific direction, students can become frustrated and overwhelmed, consequently distracting them from the purpose of the assignment.

Strategy Goal: To organize and structure content area reading assignments so students locate, learn, and remember required information

Strategy Description: Before students begin reading, provide them with a study guide or graphic organizer to complete as they read. Be sure sections of the organizer or study guide parallel the way the desired information is located in the book, as well as how it's stated or explained to provide the student with predictability and consistency. Put page numbers and/or paragraph locations so the student isn't frustrated trying to remember where details were found.

---Example---

The Importance of Satellites

For each of the following, give a definition or describe the discovery or event.

Sir Isaac Newton, 1957 (page 48)

satellite (page 49)

orbit (page 49)

Sputnik, 1957 (page 50)

What else has Earth been called? Why? (page 50)

At first, the Earth was believed to be flat. Then, it was believed to be a slightly flattened sphere. Now, through use of satellites for observation, it has been discovered the Earth is _____. (page 51)

What are some other reasons satellites are important to us? (page 52)

**Other Content Area
Reading Strategies:**

Using a highlight marker, highlight only the information that is truly essential for the student to focus on in her textbook, like key terms in a science or history book, or important people, events, or discoveries. Have any study guide or graphic organizer the student must complete parallel the highlighted information.

Let students with attention and/or reading problems use alternative materials that cover the same required concepts. For example, a student might use a high-interest computer program about Shakespeare's life and works or other print material that provides concepts in a more simplified manner. For homework purposes, arrange for the student to check out the appropriate software.

7 Enhancing comprehension

> Students with ADHD often process information slowly when they read. They need extra time to think, understand, and work so their overall comprehension skills can be used and strengthened.

Strategy Goal:

To organize reading assignments in manageable ways so students can focus effectively and then successfully complete follow-up comprehension activities

Strategy Description:

Divide a reading assignment into parts (e.g., thirds or fourths). Put a sticky note at the point where each section will end so the student knows how far to go.

On half of a worksheet, only put the reading questions corresponding to that particular reading section. The student will feel more confident and can pay attention when the assignment seems doable. Read through the questions ahead of time so the student can focus on what's important in the story or other reading material.

When the student finishes part of an assignment, she can say, "I'm ready for the next part (or set)" and feel a sense of accomplishment as she works toward the overall goal.

To help students focus more effectively, group related questions. For example, one half of a worksheet might ask only fact and opinion questions or questions that help the student analyze characters' personalities and actions.

Other Comprehension Strategies:

As the student reads, have her summarize what she remembers or complete pre-assigned questions using a voice-activated tape recorder to record answers at designated stopping points along the way. She can then listen to her tape to review story details and key concepts.

Encourage students to jot down what they think is important as they read (e.g., setting, characters, dates, a significant event). Later, when students complete comprehension activities and perhaps even quizzes, they can refer back to their notes for help. Note-taking can be used for literary materials as well as materials in content-area classes.

> Because of problems paying attention for even short periods of time, students with ADHD may exhibit difficulties in their listening comprehension abilities. They need active learning strategies to keep their attention and increase their involvement with reading material that is read aloud.

Strategy Goal: To help students increase their auditory attention and their listening comprehension during oral reading time

Strategy Description: First review or teach your students about story maps. On an overhead transparency, make a story map like the example below.

Story Map Overhead Transparency

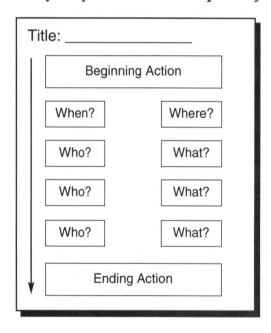

Depending on the number of characters and important events in the story, the number of *Who?* and *What?* boxes will vary as may other areas for questions or details you feel are relevant to the story.

Go through the information on the story map with an example story the class has already read. Then tell your students you will be looking for the same information in the story they are about to read. On large index cards or sheets of construction paper, make story map parts so you have manipulative story map parts. For example, one card would say *Who?* while another one would say *Where?*

Student Story Map Parts

Select students to give the cards to, particularly those who need more interaction to help their attention. Explain to each student that she is responsible for locating the information in the story. As students listen, they should jot down on the back of their cards the assigned information when they hear it. For long stories, have students offer the information at select stopping points in the reading. For short stories, they can wait until the end to share answers.

On the overhead transparency, write in the same information from the story map parts as it's contributed or afterward depending on how you use this strategy. If students are responsible for the material for testing, they can fill in their own copies of the story map later.

Other Listening Comprehension Strategies:

Note: The following strategies are adaptations of the strategy on page 150 described under Strategy Description. Be sure to read about it before you adapt this strategy for other purposes.

For older students, a story map could include terminology like the following.

- Character(s)
- Conflict(s)
- Climax
- Complication(s)
- Resolution

Make as many story cards as needed to cover the elements of the story. Older students can also look for things like foreshadowing, irony, and point of view depending on learning goals.

An overhead transparency and manipulative story map can also work for content area material. For example, as students listen to reading about a historical event or science discovery, they can complete an outline or event map. Parts for the cards and overhead transparency may include things like the following.

**Event or Discovery
Overhead Transparency**

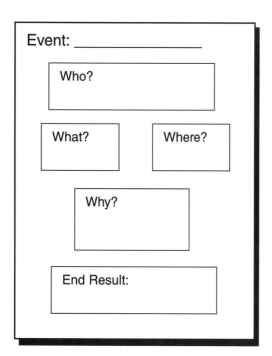

**Event or Discovery
Student Story Map Parts**

> Sometimes students with ADHD experience visual attention problems. They may need help keeping their places while reading and also knowing what is of visual importance in a reading selection.

Strategy Goal: To alert the student's attention before reading so she can focus on visual details of the material and then the actual reading itself

Strategy Description: Use a "preview time" technique before reading just like the one used before a movie in a theater. The only difference is this preview time focuses on just the one reading selection.

During the preview time, alert students to any pictures, captions, chapter titles, or other visual detail that will need to be paid attention to while reading and discuss their potential significance to the selection.

If the selection is to be read aloud, also let students know who the first readers will be so they aren't visually distracted by the process during reading. For example, you might say, "Jason and Tashonda will be reading the first page, then Nick and Branford will take the next one. I'll let you know as we go whose turn is next."

Other Focusing Strategies: For a student with visual attention problems, mark her reading spot ahead of time. Use strips of sticky note paper to mark the beginning and end of the student's section, or use the new removable highlighting tape available at office supply stores.

Use the pictures, captions, or other details to help students make predictions about the story as you preview. While reading, have students check the accuracy of their predictions.

After a page or logical section is read and the picture or other graphic with it discussed, ask students what other visual might have been used. Ask them to explain its connection to the events of the story in that particular section. For example, a story of a boy playing baseball might show the boy at bat. If this was a nervous batter worried about how he'd do, maybe a thought bubble could be used with the word "Out!" in it for representation instead.

10 Identifying and remembering important details in literature

> Students with ADHD need help selecting important details in the stories and literature they read. They also need help remembering these details.

Strategy Goal:
To help students actively interact with the literature they're reading so they can locate and remember important story details

Strategy Description:
Plan for stopping points and sharing activities as you read a story. For example, once students know the setting, main characters, and basic conflict, stop to do a sharing activity. In pairs, students can write down the facts they've learned— characters, setting, basic conflict—as well as any questions they have. Follow up the activity with a short discussion to check understanding and to answer questions.

As more complications in the plot arise, stop again and have partners share and perhaps make predictions about outcome. When you're finished reading the story, have partners again share their reactions to the outcome of the conflict and the end of the story.

Other Strategies for Remembering Story Details:
For longer literary works, show a videotape made of the literary work while reading it. For example, if you're reading Shakespeare's *Romeo and Juliet*, read one act and then show the corresponding amount in the videotape. Students will be able to visualize characters and setting better while also reviewing events. Both means of story presentation will enhance attention to detail and understanding.

Read the introductory part of the story aloud where students learn character, plot, and conflict. Then assign the rest of the reading to be done silently. As students read, have oral conferences to check understanding with those students needing help with comprehension and memory.

Have students imagine they'd make a present-day movie of the story. Let them cast the characters as well as choose the setting and any other events or revisions that would update the story. Have students share the reasons for their selections.

 Understanding graphic material like pictures, graphs, and charts

> Because of visual tracking and attention weaknesses, students with ADHD may need direct instruction and review on how to read and interpret graphic material like pictures, graphs, and charts.

Strategy Goal:

To provide the student with direct instruction and materials that help her interpret and learn from important graphic information

Strategy Description:

Make a "window" to isolate the material on the page so extraneous material doesn't interfere with the student's attention. The window can be made from cutting out space on a large index card or other stiff material.

For additional help focusing the student's attention, use color coding. For example, for a graph, you might color code the headings on the left and bottom of the window so the student can interpret the information. You can say something like, "Look at the blue highlighted information. What's happening to it as we follow the yellow highlighted information along the bottom?"

Other Strategies
for Graphic Materials:

Make a copy of the graphic so the student can isolate it for viewing and also write on it as needed. Have the student make arrows to indicate what's happening with the information. For example, for a line graph an arrow may be drawn horizontally to the right, while another one is drawn vertically going up. Review with the student the data recorded vertically and horizontally. The student can then follow the arrows to interpret the relationship between the data. Or, if the information is presented as a flowchart, the student can number the steps and add any extra explanation to help her understanding.

When referring to a graphic from a book, for example, make an overhead copy of it. Then, as you point to information on the overhead and explain, students know where to follow along in their books.

Chapter 11: Science and Social Studies

Social studies and science classes are big challenges for the student with attention deficit hyperactivity disorder (ADHD). These content areas are intensely information-laden and also involve using other sub-skills related to reading and math. When a student begins a new unit in social studies or science, he is on a quest to understand and store as much information as possible in his brain. To do so, the student must be able to acquire new vocabulary, comprehend new concepts, memorize facts, understand time concepts, interpret visual aids and diagrams, and use measurement.

Unlike reading and math where the mastery of early skills provides a foundation for acquiring later skills, each unit in social studies or science presents a totally new framework for learning. Consider how dissimilar it is to study the effects of barometric pressure one week and then to memorize different kinds of rock the next. Or how different it is to analyze the causes of the Civil War in one unit and then to remember significant dates and leaders during the Civil Rights Movement in another unit. The student must constantly adapt the kinds of reading, memory, and math skills he needs to the subject matter.

The strategies and activities in this chapter will help your students with ADHD learn more effectively in their social studies and science classes. Areas covered are listed below.

1. using math-related skills
2. building memory skills
3. acquiring content vocabulary
4. completing experiments and activities
5. reading and interpreting visual aids
6. taking and preparing for tests
7. taking notes
8. handling projects and research reports

1 Using math-related skills

Students with ADHD may have weak math and directional skills. They will need direct instruction and review of any math skills related to the social studies or science curriculum in order to succeed.

Strategy Goal: To provide the student with any math or direction skills he needs to complete an instructional activity

Strategy Description: Prior to a social studies activity (e.g., interpreting a map) or a science experiment, review or teach any related math skills that would facilitate success.

─Example─

Science

- measuring length with a ruler or meter stick
- reading degrees on a thermometer
- measuring ounces or milliliters on a cup, beaker, or test tube
- making line or bar graphs

Social Studies

- telling direction left, right, north, south, east, west
- understanding degrees of latitude and longitude on a map
- using mileage scales
- making line or bar graphs

Other Math-related Strategies:

When pairing students for activities, put a student with stronger skills with one who will need more help. Try to keep partnerships the same for many activities so the students become comfortable and can learn from each other.

If a student has extremely weak math skills, eliminate as much reliance on his math skills for the science or social studies activity as possible. For example, if the student has to measure a length of something and then cut it, have the piece already measured and prepared. Or if a student needs to construct a bar graph using population data, give the student a graph with the title and vertical and horizontal axes of the graph already filled in and have him add the data to construct the actual bar graphs.

 Building memory skills

Students with ADHD may have difficulty remembering all the facts and details presented in their content area classes. They need to learn and apply memory strategies so they can retain important facts.

Strategy Goal:

To help the student learn memory strategies for retaining new information

Strategy Description:

Using consistent formats of instructional presentation can help the student visualize and remember new information.

Whether you're giving notes or having students fill in notes or study guides about new information, have them fill out the information in ways that facilitate memory. Use graphic organizers like the following while teaching.

Chapter _____	
Famous Person or Event	
Description	
Date	
Why Important	

Other Memory Strategies:

Immediately after students read or hear about new information, have them check their memory by filling out a graphic organizer. An organizer using the 5 W's and H can quickly measure what a student remembers. Use it again for review the next day.

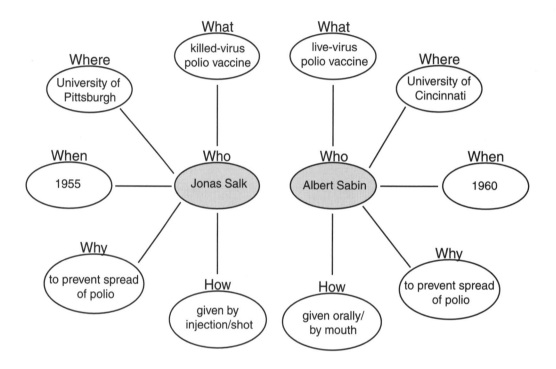

Have students make flash cards for review before quizzes and tests. Put the event, person, or term on one side and the related information on the back. Let students review as partners before tests or quizzes as well as using the flash cards to study on their own.

Students with ADHD may have difficulty acquiring and remembering new words and concepts in their content area classes. They need direct instruction of the vocabulary to help them understand the main ideas of a unit.

Strategy Goal: To help the student learn and remember new vocabulary for each unit

Strategy Description: Teach new vocabulary words based on connections, relationships, or functions as much as possible so students avoid learning words in isolation. Whenever possible, teach words or relationships of the words in a graphic or picturable manner. Use transparencies on an overhead projector as well as individual student copies for initial instruction.

Example

New Vocabulary: town, city, state, country, continent
Method of Instruction: teach by showing relationship of small to large in size as well as one being located in the other

City: Chicago
State: Illinois
Country: United States of America

New Vocabulary: nerves, neurons, dendrites, synapse
Method of Instruction: teach by diagram and by explaining the functions of each part

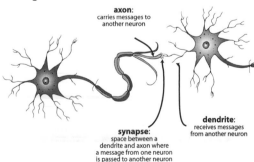

axon: carries messages to another neuron

dendrite: receives messages from another neuron

synapse: space between a dendrite and axon where a message from one neuron is passed to another neuron

Neurons are nerve cells. They make up the nerves that connect your brain to the rest of your body.

Other Vocabulary Strategies:

Instead of having students "answer the questions at the end of the section," create cloze procedure activities to reinforce vocabulary and concepts. Students are more likely to retain the information if they continue to see a word identified in a consistent manner. You may want to provide a word bank for help. The following is a small part of what might become a lengthier cloze passage.

Example

famine   drought   vegetation

A _____ occurs when there is not enough rainfall to water the _____, or plants and trees, in the area. As a result, a community may face _____ and people may not have enough to eat.

Decide which words and concepts are crucial for students to know to understand the unit. Present students with the list before beginning the unit and have them identify the words. Then have a discussion of each word, tying the new word to the students' own experiences or to concepts you know the students are familiar with.

4 ◆ Completing experiments and activities

> Instruction within the science and social studies content areas is often experiential in nature through activities, experiments, and other projects. Students with ADHD need structure and very specific directions so they can handle such experiences safely and successfully.

Strategy Goal: To prepare the student for successful experiences with hands-on activities like experiments, projects, and other activities

Strategy Description: Any activity or experiment has several "sub-directions" that are important to understand. Try to anticipate all the extra directions that will need to be spelled out for the student with ADHD. (You'll be surprised how many are helpful for "regular" kids, too!) It is helpful to provide the directions on a sheet the student can have at his table as well as a copy on the overhead as a reminder.

Here are some tips for successful experiments or partner/ group activities or projects.

1. Pair the student with ADHD with other students who will seriously complete the activity or experiment and also encourage that student's participation.

2. Divide up the activity, project, or experiment into different steps. Assign roles to partners or group members so each one knows what step(s) he or she is responsible for. Put individual directions and role responsibilities on a sheet students can refer to as they do the activity.

3. Go over any rules for materials used for the activity. Include any directions regarding handling things safely, sharing materials, and cleaning up.

4. Provide models or descriptions of what students should discover or end up with as the result of the experiment, activity, or project.

5. Set a time limit. Tell students what you expect by when. Give a five-minute warning ahead of finishing time.

Other Activity Strategies:

Be alert to any cutting, drawing, writing/typing, or other motor skills difficulties when assigning activities, experiments, or projects. Either prepare things ahead of time for the student, like having things precut or providing pictures, or create an alternative activity within the student's capability. Pairing the student with another student who has those abilities and giving the student with ADHD a different role is also an alternative.

If a student is so distractible, inattentive, or impulsive that interactive activities are too much of a risk, provide an alternative activity. Allow the student to research a related topic in the library or to complete an activity via computer that covers similar concepts. So the student doesn't feel so "singled out," allow him to have a partner or have a few students do the same activity and then share what they've learned.

 5 **Reading and interpreting visual aids**

> Students with ADHD need direct instruction and review in how to read and interpret visual aids like maps, time lines, diagrams, and graphs.

Strategy Goal:

To teach students how to read, interpret, or make visual aids to help content understanding

Strategy Description:

If a visual aid is crucial to students' understanding of a concept or needs to be created as part of an assignment, like a graph or time line, instruct students how to read it first.

Make an overhead transparency of the visual aid, copying a page from the textbook if needed. Enlarge the visual aid so it's easy for students to see. As you explain how to read the visual aid, use colored transparency markers to highlight the different information. Make sure students have their own copies to follow along at their desks.

Other Strategies for Using Visual Aids:

After reviewing an important concept by using a visual aid, present each student with a copy of a blank visual aid to fill in. Then test their understanding by asking them questions that require them to use their visual aids.

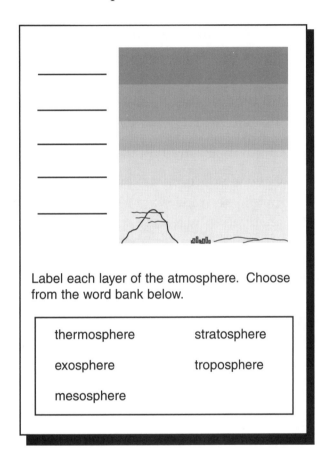

Label each layer of the atmosphere. Choose from the word bank below.

thermosphere	stratosphere
exosphere	troposphere
mesosphere	

Possible Questions:

In which layer is hail and snow formed? *troposphere*

Which layer is most affected by pollution? *stratosphere*

What is the name of the highest layer? *exosphere*

Which layer is the thinnest? *exosphere*

Keep a variety of visual aids posted around the room so students can refer to them and get used to reading them. For example, a room-sized time line can be posted when studying the events of the Civil Rights Movement, or a large flowchart diagram can be made to show the steps in photosynthesis.

6 ◆ **Taking and preparing for tests**

> Due to memory difficulties and possible associated learning
> disabilities, students with ADHD don't always test well. They
> need testing and "check for understanding" accommodations
> to best assess what they know and understand.

Strategy Goal: To provide the student with testing accommodations that fit
his individual needs and best assess his understanding and
recall

Strategy Description: Several accommodations can be used for testing that
help determine what a student actually knows without
inadvertently testing spelling or memory abilities. Use
the following tips when constructing a test or quiz.

1. Provide banks of words students can choose from when answering
   fill-in-the-blank questions. Banks can be provided for any information
   needed to be recalled and recognized. You can provide banks for fill-
   in-questions about:

   - vocabulary or concepts
   - dates
   - important people
   - important events

   Keep the amount of information in a bank reasonable so students
   aren't overwhelmed with too many choices. For example, have no
   more than 8-10 fill-in questions at a time with no more than 8-10
   choices in the bank.

2. Pare down the number of choices given at a time for a multiple-choice
   question. By keeping a maximum of three choices, the student isn't
   overwhelmed with the amount of reading or length of testing.

3. Be sure to use the same language for testing that you used when
   giving notes during instruction or from the textbook materials that
   students use. Students with ADHD often don't recognize a concept
   they know if different vocabulary is used to describe it. For example,
   if you had students list what is alike or different about a concept in
   their notes or worksheets, use the words *alike* and *different* in testing
   instead of introducing new words like *compare* and *contrast*.

4. Read directions aloud to students before the test so they understand what is being expected in each section. Keep directions short and clear.

Other Testing Strategies: Hold a conference with a student to test understanding rather than requiring formal written testing. For example, ask two thinking questions that allow the student to summarize what he's learned and use supporting facts.

For review, create practice tests that are similar to the one you'll give. Students will be prepared for the testing format as well as the knowledge they will be tested on.

For essay questions, allow the student to dictate to you or to tape record answers so writing doesn't interfere with his thought processes.

 7   **Taking notes**

Content-area subject teachers often require note-taking in class. Students with ADHD need help taking and organizing their notes so they can be used for later study.

Strategy Goal: To provide students with easy-to-follow formats for attending to and completing notes

Strategy Description: When giving notes in class, use graphic organizers to help illustrate and organize the critical concepts you want students to learn. Graphic organizers include things like flowcharts, diagrams, and charts. Graphic organizers help students remember how information was organized and thus recall it more easily.

	Examples	Where They Live	How They Breathe	How Young Are Produced
Reptiles	lizard, snake, crocodile, turtle	land	lungs	lay on land; some live birth; internal fertilization
Amphibians	frog, toad, salamander	land and water	lungs and/or gills	lay in water; internal or external fertilization

At the end of instruction, take a blank copy of the graphic organizer and review the information again, having students contribute the information. This type of review is necessary for students with ADHD who retain short amounts of information at a time.

Other Note-taking Strategies:

Any time you give notes or information, present it on an overhead projector. Provide individual copies of the notes for students so they can follow along and copy as you go. If possible, create the notes as a guide or outline that students can fill in with missing information as you discuss the notes. Having some fill-in information will help students stay attentive.

Whenever you present information through a filmstrip or videotape, prepare a note-taking study guide to go with it so students know what information to focus on. Go over the guide aloud with students. Then have them set the guide aside while they watch the videotape or filmstrip. Make sure they understand that they will have time afterward to complete it so they don't try to focus on too many tasks at a time.

8   Handling projects and research reports

Science and social studies teachers often require students to do research for reports and projects. Students with ADHD need specific directions and structure for researching, organizing information, and using it to complete an activity.

Strategy Goal: To provide organizational support that helps students research and complete a report or project successfully

Strategy Description: Use a three-step approach each time you assign a report or project so students become better organizers and planners.

1. Determine the steps of the project. First analyze the activity you're about to assign and determine how many "steps" it takes to complete.

   Ask yourself questions like, "How many days will students need to do research? How long will it take to organize and write the paper or put the project together (including computer lab time)?" and "Will students present their finished projects to the class?"

2. Develop a time line or calendar covering all steps a student needs to do with an estimate of how long each step will take. Give students copies of the time line so they can keep track of their progress.

3. Write directions and make graphic organizers so students know exactly what to do at each step. See the examples on this page and on page 170 for a project in which students create a 3D representation of the geography of a major continent.

Time Line for 3D Continent Project

Day 1:   Provide overall project directions.

          Describe or show students models of what you expect
          them to produce. Tell them what else they'll be turning in
          (e.g., their research and planning notes) as part of their
          completed project.

          Students choose continents to research.

Day 2:   Research day in the library.

Day 3:   Planning day for project. Gather materials needed today
          in class and at home. Turn in planning sheet at end of class.

Day 4:   Work day to construct project.

Day 5:   Work day to construct project.

Day 6:   Presentation day.

example time line

Notes for 3D Continent Project   Name _____

Use at least three different library sources to find the information listed below about your continent. Be sure to include your sources at the end of this note sheet.

Name of Continent

Size

Population

Kinds of Vegetation

Kinds of Mammals, Fish, and Reptiles

Bodies of Water

Land Features

Climate

Sources used to gather this information. Include information like title, author, and date whether you use books or web sites.

1.

2.

3.

example graphic organizer

3D Continent Project   Name _____

Plan your project using the chart below. Describe the geographic features you'll represent and the materials you'll need to use. Be sure to include the material for the continent itself. Use materials you can easily locate.

Geographic Feature	Materials

example planning sheet

Other Research and Project Strategies:

Some students with ADHD may be overwhelmed by the number of decisions they need to make to complete a project. Determine what is most important for the student to do himself, like researching the information for the report or project. Decide which decisions you think the student can make without becoming too overwhelmed or frustrated. For example, you may want to assign the student a particular topic and provide him with a given set of materials with which to accomplish it.

Have alternatives for any student with additional problems (e.g., reading or coordination difficulties) that may interfere with his ability to do an activity. For example, instead of constructing a 3D continent model, a student could fill in a map with its features or tell the class about his continent while pointing to a large classroom map.

Writing is a complex process for most students with attention deficit hyperactivity disorder (ADHD). Whether taking notes during a classroom lesson or generating new ideas for a paper, the student must focus on multiple processes simultaneously. He has to focus his thoughts on the topic, remember his ideas so he can write them, word his ideas appropriately, and then hand write them on paper. At any stage of the process, the student with ADHD can lose focus and become easily frustrated. And it's no wonder.

The following tips and activities will help students with ADHD handle the demands of writing as typically seen in the classroom. Writing areas covered in this chapter are listed below.

1 taking notes in the classroom

2 structuring the writing environment

3 generating creative writing

4 organizing ideas

5 spelling

6 grammar and usage

7 essay tests and questions

8 handling longer written projects and time lines

9 getting writing quality

1   Taking notes in the classroom

> Students with ADHD need extra time to process information
> and to copy it down as they take notes in the classroom.

Strategy Goal: To organize and structure classroom notes to focus student attention on important concepts

Strategy Description: Prepare either a note web or a fill-it-in outline that summarizes some of the main concepts you want students to learn. The web or outline can be open or partially completed depending on the needs of your students.

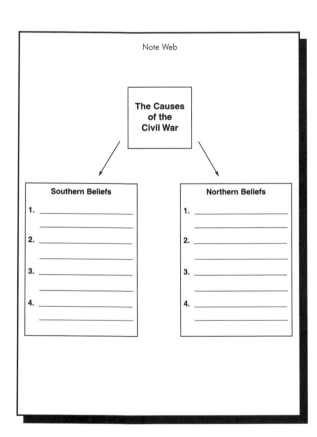

Note Web

The Causes
of the
Civil War

Southern Beliefs

1. _____
   _____
2. _____
   _____
3. _____
   _____
4. _____
   _____

Northern Beliefs

1. _____
   _____
2. _____
   _____
3. _____
   _____
4. _____
   _____

Fill-it-in Outline

Parts of Blood

I. Red Blood Cells
   A. Job (or function) _____
   B. Number _____

II. White Blood Cells
   A. Job (or function) _____
   B. Number _____

III. Platelets
   A. Job (or function) _____
   B. Number _____

IV. Plasma
   A. Job (or function) _____
   B. Amount _____

Other Note-taking Strategies:

Modify the strategy by considering how the material you want students to know can best be presented and memorized. For example, some information is best presented in chart or time line form. Let the content dictate the format.

The student can complete part of a note web or fill-it-in outline ahead of time at home, with the resource teacher, or on his own. Have the teacher tell the student what material or chapter pages will be covered a day or two ahead of time.

Audiotape the teacher's presentation (with the instructor's permission). Have the student complete as much as possible within the class time. Allow the student to listen to the tape and fill in any gaps on his note web or fill-it-in outline either at home or in a resource room or study hall.

Provide the student with paper copies of your notes from the board or overhead. To keep the student's attention focused during the presentation, have him use a highlight marker to highlight notes as they're covered. You can have the student make handwritten copies of the notes later as a form of review or if you provide credit to students for note-taking.

Allow students to copy notes before discussing them so attention isn't divided.

Have a folder or notebook available for each student for that particular class. Make available a bin or tray where all students can leave their folders or notebooks at the end of class, after they've put the day's notes in them.

Structuring the writing environment

> Students with ADHD need minimal distraction and adequate structure and direction to ensure success with written assignments.

Strategy Goal: To provide an appropriate writing environment, including the place and special materials

Strategy Description: Provide a special spot in the classroom just for producing written assignments. This place can be for any of your students who require more help focusing their energies, whether they are writing answers to a fill-in worksheet or completing a lengthier written assignment.

You might have a spot with study carrels or a table and chairs placed behind movable dividers. You might also consider letting the student decorate his spot. We all tend to do better when we're comfortable.

Other Writing Strategies: For students with motor skill difficulties, provide wider-lined paper. Students may also need pencils with grippers or larger pencils or pens. (Make sure you don't provide too many choices to add to the distraction!)

Provide assistive technology to facilitate handwriting and attention. Allow students to dictate an assignment into a tape recorder or to use a computer for word processing.

Let the student dictate his assignment to a writing buddy. Then the pair can review the quality of writing together. Allow both students to share and improve their assignments.

Place a written copy of the assignment directions in front of the student. A written check-off list with assignment criteria can also help ensure completion.

Give the student a sample model of what you want the assignment to look like and include when it is to be completed.

3 Generating creative writing

> When students with ADHD are provided with assignments of a more creative nature, they can be easily overwhelmed and distracted by having too much choice.

Strategy Goal: To help guide the student's thinking as he organizes thoughts for a creative writing assignment

Strategy Description: Develop key questions related to the goal of your assignment as a way to guide thinking. Let the "answers" to the questions guide further paragraph development. For example, require that each question be answered with three or four sentences of explanation (supporting details).

Set aside one-on-one time to help individual students with key questions, if they are allowed to make their own topic choices.

─Example─

Topic: How to Play Basketball

Key Question 1: What is the game of basketball?

Key Question 2: Where is the game played and what equipment is used?

Key Question 3: What are the rules for playing basketball?

Other Creative Writing Strategies: Present the student with two or three topic choices to choose from.

To get the student's ideas flowing freely, let him dictate into a tape recorder, to another student, or to the teacher. Later the student can listen and transcribe his thoughts and make any necessary changes.

Use a kitchen timer to get a student going. For example, tell the student he must write nonstop for ten minutes on a given or free choice topic to meet the assignment requirements for the day.

Set a minimum criteria, like the number of sentences or lines per day, to get students to write.

Use journal writing on a regular basis. When it's time to produce a longer, more polished work, allow the student to choose a journal topic upon which to expand.

 4 ## Organizing ideas

> Students with ADHD need help choosing logical ways to organize and complete their writing.

Strategy Goal:
To provide students with organizational choices for focusing their writing

Strategy Description:
Give students a number of topics to choose from when you give a writing assignment. With each topic, also suggest ways to organize their ideas. Let the type of content for the writing guide organizational suggestions. Some organizational methods include:

- chronological (e.g., first to last, newest to oldest)
- space or location (e.g., up to down, front to back, left to right)
- give three examples
- give four reasons
- easiest to most difficult
- list the steps

Then students can brainstorm using their organizational methods.

┌─ Example ──────────────────────────

Topic: If you became the principal, describe three things you would change about your school.

Ways to organize: Most important to least important; or first, second, third

Brainstorming

   Most Important: Longer passing time between classes

   Next most important: Better food at lunch

   Least important (but still important): No PE classes

Other Organizational Strategies:

When students brainstorm or write rough drafts, have them write individual ideas or sentences on strips of paper. Then have the students take the strips and put them in a logical order. The order can then guide their final written copy.

Provide pre-written short introductions for topics that suggest methods of organizing as well as other ideas. Let students choose introductions and finish organizing and writing. Two students might get the same topic and later compare their finished products.

As a class, take one topic and lead the class through all the ways someone might organize their thinking to write a paper. Write ideas on the board and have students copy them as examples to guide them in their writing.

Spelling

Students with ADHD may have problems associated with visual and/or auditory memory. Consequently, their ability to recognize and remember correct spellings is affected.

Strategy Goal: To facilitate auditory and/or visual memory of correct spellings by grouping or teaching words in meaningful ways

Strategy Description: Combine modalities when teaching and reviewing spelling. The following two methods might be effective.

- Make large individual letter cards that students can arrange to make correct spellings. Students can refer to a list, then "spell" each word using the cards. You might then test the students by having them spell the words using the cards without referring to the list.

- Have students visually exaggerate and emphasize trouble areas in words using highlight colors or by varying the size of letters.

wri**T**ing   enou**gh**

Other Spelling Strategies: Through observation and possible pretesting, determine a student's primary method of learning to spell, such as visual memorizing, auditory/phonetic connecting, or writing and checking. Prepare lessons that use the student's strengths and learning styles.

Provide word patterns for memory, like grouping words by common endings or by themes.

Combine spelling and vocabulary study by providing one single list for both. When testing, test for both correct spelling and knowledge of word meaning.

Use alternative testing methods. For example, for more auditory learners, let students dictate word spellings into a tape recorder or to a partner who will write each dictated word and then show the student the spelling. For visual learners, create a test with three possible spellings to choose from for each word. Students circle the correct spelling. Allow students to use inventive spelling on first drafts of writing projects. Then go over the project with the student and correct any misspellings together. Point out any patterns in misspellings. A possible list for further study might be created from these words.

 6 ◆ **Grammar and usage**

Students with ADHD may have problems with grammar and usage like subject-verb agreement and word endings because of inattention to details.

Strategy Goal:

To help focus students' attention on appropriateness and correctness of language, usage, and expression of ideas

Strategy Description:

"Warm up" the student with related practice before he looks for language and usage correctness in his own work. If possible, secure samples of the student's writing ahead of time from a previous year's teacher or another content area teacher. Analyze the student's writing for patterns of errors. Then create two or three different practice items so the student has concrete examples of what to look for in his own writing.

───Example───

For the student who leaves off verb endings:

1. The dealer pass out six cards to each player. (passes)
2. When all the cards have been dealt, each player pick two more cards from the center pile. (picks)

For the student who leaves out words:

1. Jeremy kicked the ball Matt and ran down the sideline toward the goal. (to Matt)
2. Good math teachers show students to work out a problem before they assign them on their own. (how to work out)

Other Language and Usage Strategies:

In a quiet, distraction-free setting, have the student read his writing aloud to you. Have the student listen and decide if what he says "sounds" correct. Together, you may listen for things like missing words, repeated words, missing word endings, incomplete ideas, or incorrectly expressed ideas. For more mature writers, check for the level of complexity of language and the use of slang or informal language.

Students with ADHD may have social difficulties and consequently may not express themselves appropriately on paper either. For example, they may take direction liberally and literally when asked to express an opinion about something, ranting and raving more than explaining and reasoning logically. Or they may choose words that are not appropriate to use in a classroom setting. If this describes your student, check in periodically to see what he's writing. If there are problems, privately conference with the student, showing him how to express the same ideas in a more appropriate way.

A student with ADHD may write in a simple way to get the assignment done, regardless of quality or appropriateness for grade level. Encourage a student to "upgrade" his writing wherever needed by asking, "What's another way to say this?" Hopefully, you can elicit more sophisticated vocabulary and wording in the process. Accept the result as sufficient revision for this student's papers.

7   **Essay tests and questions**

During any kind of testing, students with ADHD usually need more time. Essay tests and questions, in particular, take longer because of the amount of planning, organizing of ideas, and writing required.

Strategy Goal: To help the student plan and write essay question answers within a reasonable amount of time

Strategy Description: Give students the question ahead of time so they can brainstorm and organize ideas before committing thoughts to paper. Create a planning sheet for brainstorming and recording ideas. Write the question to answer on the planning sheet.

---Example---

A. Essay Question: Why and in what ways is it important to take care of your skin?

B. Brainstorm your ideas below. Write down everything you know about the topic.

> Use sunscreen—it protects against sunburn and skin cancer.
> Wash cuts—skin is the first line of defense against disease and germs.
> Keep clean—prevents body odor; friends will like you.
> Use lotion—it replaces lost skin oil; prevents dryness and cracking of skin in cold weather

C. Organize your answer below in the order you think you'll write it. You'll need to explain each of your brainstormed ideas with several more sentences.

Remember: Take this paper with you. You can use it on the test!

Other Essay Writing Strategies:

Allow students to dictate answers or to shorthand answers and to follow up with a verbal explanation of ideas to the teacher later on.

To practice the thinking and organizing required to answer essay questions, substitute short essay questions for oral discussion of a class topic. Give students a follow-up topic to a class lesson and have them each write a short essay answer. Then have students share their essays in small groups, pairs, or with the class.

Provide a fill-in framework for students to organize and "write" essay answers. The example on the next page is for a short story or novel essay question.

---Example---

Essay Direction: Give a brief description of the plot.

Fill-in Answer

1. At the beginning of the story, we met the main characters
   _____ and _____.

2. The main conflict in the story was between _____
   and _____ because _____
   _____.

3. Several problems occurred as the plot moved along. They were
   _____, _____,
   and _____.

4. The most exciting part of the story was when _____
   _____
   _____.

5. The story finally ended with _____
   _____
   _____.

> When students with ADHD (and even those without) are given "work time" in class or a project that extends over several days outside the classroom, little may actually get accomplished. They may be unable to plan for the appropriate amount of time needed or to break down steps leading to completion of the larger project.

Strategy Goal: To help students plan and break a larger project into subtasks with specific directions and time lines

Strategy Description: Obtain directions and time lines ahead of time for projects in other content areas. First divide the directions into manageable chunks for understanding and accomplishment. Then sit down with the student and problem solve/negotiate how to complete the project. Be sure to build in time for any accommodations, like extended time in meeting time lines or a proofing step by the teacher before the assignment is turned in.

─Example─────────

Social Studies

Assignment: Choose a famous figure in the Civil Rights Movement. Write a one-page typed paper describing this person's contribution to civil rights as we understand them today. Use two different sources for your information. The assignment will be due _____.

Writing Plan

Step 1:   Choose a famous figure in civil rights. To be completed by _____.

Step 2:   Research the person using the Internet and take notes. To be completed by _____.

Step 3:   Research the person using other library sources and take notes. To be completed by _____.

Step 4:   Write the rough draft. Include the person's background and accomplishments. To be completed by _____.

Step 5:   Share my rough draft with my resource teacher and classroom teacher. To be completed by _____.

Step 6: Type my paper and include any changes based on comments from my teachers. To be completed by _____.

Step 7: Conference with one of my teachers to proof my paper. To be completed by _____.

Step 8: Turn in my typed, final copy. To be completed by _____.

Other Planning Strategies: As an incentive, give the student a grade or points for each section or step of a project he completes. Then give a grade for overall quality and meeting of assignment criteria.

Build a work time grade into project grading criteria. You might give the student points each work day for being on-task.

Make a visual time line as a reminder to the student. Each time he completes a project step, the student can color in or extend the time line.

Example

- ❑ Day 1 ———— Pick my topic and brainstorm in writing.

- ❑ Day 2 ———— Write my introduction.

- ❑ Day 3 ———— Write two body paragraphs.

- ❑ Day 4 ———— Write my conclusion.

- ❑ Day 5 ———— Proofread my paper and type it.

- ❑ Day 6 ———— Turn in my final typed paper.

Let students organize thoughts aloud as you record and organize them on paper. Then have the students turn the information into sentences and paragraphs.

Getting writing quality

> Students with ADHD need specific, concrete guidelines to produce complete, good quality written work.

Strategy Goal:

To help students recognize and apply the principles of quality written work

Strategy Description:

Though we would prefer that students think on their own and judge if their own written work is of good quality, many still just do the assignment to get it done.

Set minimum criteria for the type of written work you'll find acceptable for a particular assignment. Spell out the criteria you feel are most important for the assignment. Assignments can range from daily work where you may have consistent criteria to longer assignments with varying criteria. Make sure students have written copies of the criteria to refer to as they write. Criteria might include the following.

- Three well-supported reasons or examples

- Five sentences per paragraph

- Minimum of five paragraphs

- All sentences should begin with a capital letter and end with punctuation.

- Research resources must include information from 1998 or more recent.

- Number of pages and whether typed or written

- Blue or black ink

- Neat, lined paper

Don't waiver from your established criteria just because a student finally "does" an assignment.

Other Strategies for Producing Quality:

Give students a following-directions grade as part of their overall grade. Encourage students to self-evaluate their written work according to guidelines and revise accordingly before turning in written work.

Allow students opportunities for improving grades. Students can have you review their assignments with them individually before turning them in. You might also use hand stampers or stickers with comments like "Work in Progress" or "Good Work!" For example, if a student gets a "Work in Progress" message, he can have one more day to improve the assignment.

Create grading rubrics for more extensive written assignments. Rubrics should include the most important criteria for a quality assignment. Keep criteria to a minimum, like five criteria, so students can learn from grading. For future assignments, you may want to keep some criteria the same across assignments.

Personal Narrative Paper			
	Well Written	Adequate	Needs Work
Clear Beginning, Middle, and End			
Use of Character Dialogue			
Vivid Sensory Detail (sight, taste, touch, smell, sound)			
Grammar, Spelling, Punctuation			
	___ /10	___ /10	___ /10

Chapter 13: Physical Education

Physical activity provided through physical education classes, after-school sports activities, and recess can be beneficial outlets for students with attention deficit hyperactivity disorder (ADHD). Many students with ADHD are highly skilled athletically and well-coordinated. However, social, behavioral, and attention issues sometimes interfere with a student's success in these areas.

The strategies and suggestions in this chapter will help students with ADHD succeed in the areas related to physical education, recess, and sports involvement. The areas addressed are listed below.

1 following game rules and oral directions

2 appropriate behavior and social interaction

3 meeting skill expectations

4 participating in after-school sports

Following game rules and oral directions

> The impulsivity exhibited by many students with ADHD may cause them to begin activities without getting directions or instructions first. Providing some predictability in activity structure and routine will improve a student's ability to focus attention appropriately.

Strategy Goal: To provide a predictable routine or schedule so the student is "settled" before giving directions and beginning activities

Strategy Description: Establish both a weekly and daily class routine. Create a large weekly or monthly calendar that tells students what games and activities to expect and post it in a readily visible spot. When students enter a given activity or exercise area, have them follow rules to get them ready to listen and follow directions.

─Example─

- Check the weekly schedule so you know the activity for the day.
- Sit facing forward in two horizontal rows one behind the other.
- Leave equipment in the equipment area until your teacher (or coach) tells you to get it.

Other Physical Education Strategies: For game rules, make a large, portable poster to mount in the gym area or outside. When a student needs reminding, refer her attention to the poster by saying, "Julia, remember to follow rule #2 now."

Pair oral directions with written directions and diagrams.

Create individual copies of directions and rules for students needing more review and preparation. Provide copies to students a day or two ahead of time so parents or the resource teacher can review with them in advance.

2 Appropriate behavior and social interaction

> Because a PE classroom or sports field is relatively "unstructured" compared to a classroom environment, students with ADHD need concrete behavioral expectations and rules for interaction.

Strategy Goal: To help the student learn appropriate social behavior during physical activities

Strategy Description: Provide as many concrete descriptors as possible for students' behavior during given activities. To encourage patience during turn-taking, for example, give students different colored pieces of paper. Whenever you call out a new color, the student with that colored piece of paper takes her turn.

To minimize unnecessary rowdiness or physical contact between students, establish space limits reasonable for the activity. For example, students may need to stay two feet away from each other during sit-ups.

Other Physical Education Strategies: Prepare the student for transitions to different activities. Take the student aside and review what the new activity is and what behaviors you expect during that time.

Determine consequences ahead of time for inappropriate behavior. Consequences need to be consistent and immediate to affect behavior change. For example, a student who is distracting others can be asked to sit down where she is until she's ready to listen and join in again.

Provide an exercise buddy for the student who reviews the activity rules and behavior with the student.

Some students with ADHD may need skill expectations adjusted
due to skill, coordination, hyperactivity, or attention difficulties.

Strategy Goal: To determine appropriate skill objectives within a physical
education setting

Strategy Description: While writing an IEP or Section 504 plan, make sure that the
student's needs in the areas of physical education and sports
are also accommodated. Look at the overall plan of activities
and skill expectations for students for the semester and/or
school year. For example, whereas most students may have
a list of 10-20 skills to master for swimming credit, a student
with ADHD may only be able to master putting her head
in the water and learning the front crawl. Make sure an
agreement has been made between the PE teacher and the
student about expectations ahead of time.

**Other Physical
Education Strategies:** Substitute an alternative activity for the student. For example,
allow the student to walk or run a given number of laps on the
track instead of playing soccer. To avoid making the student
feel isolated, let another student participate with her.

Pair or group students for activities based on their strengths
and needs. For example, during baseball, one student could
hit while another runs bases.

Participating in after-school sports

Students with ADHD may have interests in competitive sports and other after-school activities. Due to social, behavioral, and/or attention difficulties, however, their physical abilities and possible contribution to a team may be overlooked.

Strategy Goal: To facilitate the involvement of a student with ADHD in sports by preparing the coach and student

Strategy Description: Meet individually with the coach to share the student's interest and needs. Share what you know about the student's needs and abilities. For example, the student may need individual directions immediately following the ones given to the group to check for understanding. Or the coach may need to stand near the student to ensure that the student is looking at him and paying attention before he gives instructions.

Follow up with a meeting between you, the coach, and the student to discuss how to handle the student's needs and involvement.

Other Physical Education Strategies: Encourage students to be active in many aspects of sports. For example, many teams need a manager to handle equipment, someone to keep game statistics, or someone to videotape games.

Coordinate skill practice between the student's PE class or recess and the sport. For example, a student needing to practice passing for soccer may do so as a recess or PE activity.

Chapter 14: Communicating with Parents

Let's face it. Attention deficit hyperactivity disorder (ADHD) is a condition that affects a child 24/7. Every day, 365 days a year, he wakes up and goes to sleep with ADHD. And who knows that best? His parents.

For the child to have a productive, happy life, his condition needs to be managed with the utmost care and commitment from a large team of individuals. At the core of that team are its most crucial team members—the child's parents. They are the people who help manage a complex program which addresses the medical and physical needs of the child, who follow through on behavioral and academic plans at home, and who oversee the psychological well-being of their child. Consequently, it is very important that communication between school and home be ongoing and productive.

Here are some things to understand about parents so communication can be most effective.

1. Parents will range in levels of acceptance of the condition from unconditional acceptance to complete denial, whether the child is 6 or 26!

2. Parents will have varying amounts of time, energy, and stamina for dealing with their child.

3. Parents will have varying levels of understanding about the condition.

4. Parents will have varying expectations for their child.

5. Parents will have varying expectations of the school and you.

6. Parents will vary in involvement levels from "out of sight, out of mind" to daily monitoring (and possible over-monitoring!).

7. Parents will have varying levels of trust in you as a team member.

Role as Teacher

By now, with so many variations in parents, you're likely wondering how you can possibly know what your role is from one minute to the next. This one consistency among all parents may help guide you.

All parents care about their child and truly want to work with you.

With that as the major guideline, your role is defined as follows:

To Listen Parents can be keen observers of what works best for their child as well as what frustrates him most. Sometimes, because ADHD is such a pervasive condition, parents also need to vent and may need to bounce ideas off you for a second opinion.

To Educate Parents need to understand that ADHD is a neurophysiological disorder that affects their child's behavior, social skills, academic skills, and self-esteem. It is **not** the result of bad parenting on their part and there is much that can be done to improve the life of their child. Their child will also be consistently inconsistent—a major frustration for them until they accept that fact.

Inform the parents of current literature about medication and treatment as well as behavioral and educational techniques. Treat the parents as you would other professionals on the team who need more information about ADHD to understand it and be effective team members.

To Encourage You think dealing with the child in the classroom is tough stuff sometimes? Try being his parent! As much as possible, do what you can to keep the child-parent interaction positive on the home front. When you communicate, keep the focus neutral. Focus on the positives and the improvements rather than painting the picture of a child who presents one problem after another.

To Suggest and Recommend It is your job to keep up with current behavioral and educational techniques. You may also want to keep informed of new medications and medical treatments. Some of these new techniques and treatments may be ones the parents may wish to try with their child. However, particularly with medication and its physical effects, you are only in a position to suggest and recommend things that might work.

To Inform of Legal Rights In the early phases of an ADHD diagnosis, the process can be pretty confusing for parents. Make them aware of the kinds of testing and observation used to collect information on their child, and who will be providing such information. When a diagnosis is made, they will also need your help understanding the difference between an Individual Education Plan (IEP) and a 504 plan and which, if any, their child qualifies for.

To Refer The school can't do everything for the student with ADHD, and neither can the parents. There will be times when it is appropriate to call upon other resources. For example, the student may be experiencing severe social and psychological problems and need the help of a qualified therapist. Or an older student may be ready to graduate and need to know his resources for employment and education as an individual with ADHD in his community. Your role is to make the parents aware of all resources available at school, as well as other professionals and agencies within the community who can meet their child's needs.

Communication Tips

As the "coordinator" of a multidisciplinary team handling the needs of the student with ADHD, you will be communicating with the student's parents on a regular basis. You will want to set up routines that keep the communication flowing between home and school. General tips to help that flow of communication be most effective in meeting the student's needs are covered below. (For specific tips and strategies related to academic and behavioral needs, see Chapter 15: Providing Academic Support at Home, pages 196-204, and Chapter 16: Fostering Appropriate Behavior at Home and at School, pages 205-214.)

1. Begin the flow of team communication at the beginning of the school year and at the beginning of each semester for older students. Meet with the parents, his teachers, the school nurse, the school psychologist, the guidance counselor, and the student, if appropriate. Describe the student's needs and the goals established in his IEP or 504 plan. At the meeting, determine the level of and kind of communication needed with each team member. If the student is adjusting to a new school environment, like making the transition from middle school to high school, you may want to meet more often to ensure the student's adjustment is going smoothly.

2. Involve the school nurse and keep her informed. The school nurse may have a closer relationship with the student than anyone else, especially if the student is taking medications. The nurse will be aware of any health issues as well as stresses the student is facing, particularly if they see each other on a daily basis.

3. Make the student a member of the team. As soon as it's appropriate, invite the student to team meetings to discuss his academic and behavioral needs and progress. Even if the student is not yet mature enough to handle sitting in a team meeting, he must be involved in some way. All the behavioral plans and academic strategies in the world won't work unless the student understands the possible positive effects and agrees to actively participate.

4. Any team member should feel free to communicate directly to the parent. Everyone knows school is an extremely busy place and it's very inefficient for two people to do the same job. However, since you're most likely in the position of coordinating academic and behavioral plans for the student, be sure to stay in the loop. Ask other team members to jot you a quick note or e-mail, or to leave a short phone message summarizing the nature of any parent communication.

5. Give parents information they can act on. As you get to know the student's parents, you'll develop a sense of what they understand and how much they'll follow through on. Appropriate times to communicate are when you need the parent to reinforce your efforts or to be aware of positive progress with their child.

Chapter 15: Providing Academic Support at Home

Homework—the dreaded word in the vocabulary of any student, particularly the student with attention deficit hyperactivity disorder (ADHD). Homework conjures up negative memories of lost, late, inaccurate, or incomplete assignments. Just one more thing adding to the frustration and feelings of failure experienced by the student with ADHD.

Homework does have a legitimate purpose for the student. In general, homework helps all students take responsibility for their learning. Whether the student is in school, on the job, or dealing with life issues, she will need to know how to learn. The issue of homework, then, must be handled very carefully with each student's particular needs in mind.

What is homework?

In figuring out how to best approach homework for a particular student, it's important to look at what teachers view as its purpose and why it's important. Homework can serve a variety of functions like:

- finishing work not completed in class
- doing an individualized assignment
- reinforcing and practicing academic skills
- helping a student develop good work habits and study skills
- preparing the student with background for upcoming units and lessons

As you look at the list of purposes, it becomes clear that many of the homework assignments students receive fulfill several purposes at once. For example, reading a chapter in science and completing questions can give a student background for the next unit or chapter. It may also help a student practice content area reading and learn strategies for remembering content area concepts, a valuable study skill.

What skills are required to do homework?

That's a question teachers should ask themselves whenever they create homework assignments for a student. Being able to do homework is a more complex task than most of us would believe. It is a particularly complex task considering that we expect students to do homework independently day after day. As you look at the list of skills on the next page, think about students you know who have ADHD.

Homework requires students to have adequate skills in the areas of:

- reading and writing
- note-taking
- self-management and self-discipline
- organizational skills
- time-management skills

What happens to the quality or quantity of homework when any one of these skill areas is weak? It suffers. That is the dilemma faced by the student with ADHD who may lack several of these skills.

What about homework for the student with ADHD?

Not assign it! How about that?! There would be one fewer battle for you and other teachers, one fewer stress for the parent, and fewer frustrations for the student. Nice in theory, but it's hardly realistic and it avoids what should be a reasonable expectation for all students in school. The best way to approach homework for the student with ADHD is based on two premises:

- that the kind of homework assigned is appropriate for the individual student

- that the teacher, parent, and student work together as a team with clearly defined roles to help the student learn and apply homework skills

What is the role of the teacher?

The main role of the teacher is to ensure that the kind and amount of homework expected of a student is appropriate and reasonable and doesn't in any way penalize the student for her disability. Depending on the nature of programming for the student with ADHD, the "teacher" can be any one of her regular education teachers or her special education teacher. Excellent opportunities exist during the IEP meeting or the creation of a 504 plan to address the student's needs regarding homework as they apply to each of her classes.

The teacher's role should be to:

- give assignments that are tailored to the student's level of "homework" skills

- provide clear directions for assignments. This may include underlining or highlighting key direction words with the student and checking her understanding before she leaves for the day.

- determine an amount of work appropriate for what the student can do and that will show the teacher what she needs to know about the student

- create an assignment appropriate to a student's individual needs. Homework should not be busy work but used to develop a student's particular skill or to teach or review a concept.

- give parents timely feedback about any problem the student is having with homework so the problem doesn't lead to student failure

- facilitate completion of homework by providing the student with materials like extra copies of books, a tape recorder, or access to a computer for word processing

- help create and implement any extra homework accommodation the student might need

What are some possible homework accommodations?

Accommodations can be as varied and few as the student's needs dictate. Here are some typical accommodations.

- decreasing the amount of homework. For example, a student might be assigned half the math problems as long as she can show she knows the process.

- providing extra time for a homework assignment. This type of accommodation might be particularly helpful for longer assignments or projects that require more steps.

- giving the student a weekly calendar of assignments for a class with clear directions included. Knowing the expectations for the week and having an individual copy can help the student manage her time better to complete work.

- grading the student's work on content. Things such as spelling or appearance of the homework shouldn't penalize the student as long as the work fulfills its purpose.

- allowing the student to do her homework in a different way. The student might tape record her assignment or dictate her answers to someone else. Or the student might demonstrate or do a project as an alternative method of completing an assignment.

- giving the student an alternative textbook or other learning materials that teach the same concepts. For example, the student might have a copy of a textbook where the main concepts or core reading passages are color highlighted to reduce the amount of reading.

What is the student's role?

Bottom line, the student's role is to do the homework independently. Once homework accommodations have been provided and assignments have been designed to meet the student's individual needs, the student should be able to complete them. The role of the teacher and the role of the parents is to facilitate the homework process for the student by making assignments reasonable and conditions favorable for work. However, a student at any age must do her own work.

The student has the following responsibilities in the homework process:

- deciding when and where homework will be done
- developing a homework plan that requires no monitoring or reminders
- bringing home the necessary materials to do the homework
- asking the parent or teacher for help
- completing the assignment on time
- ensuring the assignment is legible and accurate
- handing in the assignment

What is the parent's role?

Admittedly, the role of the parent is a tough one. The parent needs to be present for the student when needed, but not so overly involved as to compromise the student's independence. The parent has to be supportive while also trying to keep the parent-child relationship a positive one. And the role of the parent only increases in complexity when the child is in the upper grades and has more teachers involved.

Success of the parent role relies on the commitment of the parent and the student together to follow through with decisions and plans.

Parents can best support their child's efforts to do homework independently by:

- providing a good study environment for the student. There should be few distractions and it should be comfortable and conducive to working.
- providing the basic study materials (e.g., pen, pencil, paper, calculator, access to a computer)
- giving the student tools for self-management when she's ready (e.g., clock, timer, calendar, daily planner)
- helping the student decide the day and time to do the homework
- being available for help when the student requests it
- periodically checking that the student is working without monitoring too closely so that the student can develop independent work habits
- following up on an agreed-upon homework plan with positive and negative consequences

- letting the teacher know about any homework problems or needs (e.g., the need for more accommodations, the teaching of specific homework skills like organization, tutoring in content areas)

- helping but not teaching. Teaching is what teachers are for. If a parent finds himself teaching, that's a signal that more direct instruction in a skill or content area by the student's teacher needs to happen.

The handouts on pages 201-204 will help the parent and student create a homework plan and monitor its success on a regular basis. Suggested directions and ways to use the handouts are provided below.

Homework Plan (page 201) The Homework Plan is an overall plan describing the process the student will use on a regular basis to complete homework as independently as possible. The Homework Plan is like a contract or agreement between the parent and student and includes the steps of the plan and any rewards or negative consequences associated with it. Like any other "contract," periodically revisit the Homework Plan as the student develops independence and becomes more responsible.

My Weekly Homework Chart (page 203) This sheet is designed for younger students and tracks a week-long period since the younger students may have fewer teachers and fewer homework assignments.

When the student finishes an assignment, she can put a check mark in the Done column. Then the parent, together with the student, checks the assignment for accuracy and puts a signature or initials in the Checked Over column.

Homework Sheet (page 204) The Homework Sheet is designed for older students or for students who are well on their way to independently monitoring their own assignment completion. An individual sheet can be used each day for all assignments, having the student transfer assignment directions from an assignment notebook to the sheet. If the student can remember to bring the sheet to and from school, she can use it instead of an assignment notebook.

The Checked for Accuracy column has been included because there's a greater expectation of this happening for older students. Hopefully, the student will check her own assignment for accuracy, or if needed, consult with her parent or teacher before handing the assignment in.

_____ 's Homework Plan

Keep the following tips in mind as you make your homework plan.

- Make a plan you and your parents can stick with.
- Leave room for flexibility. Sometimes circumstances change from one day to the next.
- Decide when and where you'll work. Leave room for a break between sessions.
- Set goals each day for your homework.
- Make a list of the smaller tasks you need to do to complete an assignment. Go over this with a parent, if needed.
- Each day, estimate how long each assignment will take.
- Decide how to get assignments home and then back to school.
- Decide on rewards for completing your work and negative consequences when you don't complete it. Also decide when you will receive those rewards and consequences.

Where I'll work: _____

I'll do my homework from _____ to _____ each evening.

I'll take a break at _____.

I will make sure assignments get home and back to school _____

_____.

I will receive a reward when _____.

I will receive a negative consequence when _____.

Rewards include:

_____

_____

Negative consequences include:

_____

_____

_____
Date

_____   _____
Student Signature   Parent Signature

Justin _____ 's Homework Plan

Keep the following tips in mind as you make your homework plan.

- Make a plan you and your parents can stick with.
- Leave room for flexibility. Sometimes circumstances change from one day to the next.
- Decide when and where you'll work. Leave room for a break between sessions.
- Set goals each day for your homework.
- Make a list of the smaller tasks you need to do to complete an assignment. Go over this with a parent, if needed.
- Each day, estimate how long each assignment will take.
- Decide how to get assignments home and then back to school.
- Decide on rewards for completing your work and negative consequences when you don't complete it. Also decide when you will receive those rewards and consequences.

Where I'll work: _at the kitchen table_

I'll do my homework from _6:00_ to _8:00_ each evening.

I'll take a break at _7:00 for 10 minutes_.

I will make sure assignments get home and back to school _in my backpack which I'll keep by the door_.

I will receive a reward when _I do my homework 2 days in a row_.

I will receive a negative consequence when _I don't do my homework 2 days in a row_.

Rewards include:

playing video games, a movie on the weekend, having a friend stay overnight

Negative consequences include:

no TV, no going out Friday night

October 5
Date

____Justin____
Student Signature

____Mrs. Kathy James____
Parent Signature

My Weekly Homework Chart

Name _____

Day	Assignment	Done	Checked Over
Monday			
Tuesday			
Wednesday			
Thursday			
Friday			
Weekend			

Chapter 15: Providing Academic Support at Home

The ADHD Companion

Homework Sheet

Name _____

Quickly review these reminders before you start your homework today.

- Check that you have all the materials you need (food included!).
- Plan how long each assignment will take.
- Stay focused and work as independently as you can.
- Record each assignment in the chart below.
- Take a very short break between assignments.

IMPORTANT!!!! When you're done, put your assignments where you'll find them the next day so you can turn them in.

Assignment	Finished Completely	Checked for Accuracy	Handed In

JR enters the Biology classroom, army camouflage jacket flapping open. He plops his overfilled book bag on the table and heads for the rats in the cage at the side of the room. (Both the coat and the bag are forbidden in our classrooms, but the Biology teacher and I overlook it. It's one fewer thing JR has to remember and we have to remind him about — if only the book bag held completed assignments.) He kids with the teacher while he pokes his finger in the rat cage, hoping one will nibble and create the drama of attention he's looking for. Done giving the rats their daily thrill, he scoots to his seat just before the bell rings.

Throughout the class time, JR listens attentively, not taking a single note or pulling out an assignment to check when the rest of the class does so. However, he certainly knows the answers when class discussion takes place. He exhibits no outward behavior problems in the classroom, except for occasionally turning around or talking with a peer behind him. If needed, a quick look from me (and a smiling nod of acknowledgment from him) gets him back on track. Getting assignments done is a whole other story. We tackle that during a study period later in the day.

Other students find JR a curiosity. He can act immature but at the same time entertain them with his keen sense of humor. JR is very articulate and probably more intelligent than many other students in the room, but his class work and grades don't prove it.

JR is 16 and he isn't taking medication, although he's been on a series of different ones for several years, some more effective than others. His dad and stepmom have given up the daily battle of forcing him to take medication (this often happens during adolescence). They are dealing with JR's other behavioral and emotional issues that are impacting the family.

And yet, day after day, JR comes to school and he survives. He keeps trying, in his own way, to succeed. Some days he is fatigued by the effort to stay tuned in, to attempt some schoolwork, to battle the frustration he feels. JR tries to please his teachers, he wants to please his parents, and he wants to make friends.

JR is truly heroic; he's a combatant of all the other issues that result from or accompany his attention deficit hyperactivity disorder (ADHD). Students like JR often:

- make impulsive decisions
- display weak social skills
- overreact to sensory stimuli
- exhibit low self-esteem
- have learning difficulties

These behaviors affect the student's classroom and home behavior and social acceptance by his peers.

Creating a working partnership between parents and teachers is crucial to helping students with ADHD improve their:

- social and behavior skills
- decision-making and problem-solving skills
- responsibility and independence

In the pages that follow, parent and teacher tips are provided to help students learn appropriate behavior. Forms for implementing strategies and behavior plans are also included for the student, teacher, and parent. If parents and teachers work closely together, students with ADHD can gain acceptance in and out of the classroom.

Tips for Fostering Appropriate Behavior in Students with ADHD

⇨ Surround the student with positive role models for behavior. Students with ADHD want social acceptance — they want to fit in. With positive role models around them, they'll learn how.

⇨ A student with ADHD needs extra time to process information and to think whether it concerns his behavior or academic performance. Give directions slowly and check the student's understanding along the way by asking him to paraphrase what you've said.

⇨ Ask the student what will help. Make sure the student understands what ADHD is and how it affects him. Solicit his expert opinion on his own needs and what may help him focus and behave more appropriately.

⇨ A student with ADHD does get restless and can, consequently, cause a disruption. To avoid the disruption and meet the student's needs, allow the student movement. You may want to develop a plan where he subtly signals his need to leave the room (e.g., to get a drink) or allow him to stretch and pace in the back of the room as long as he returns to his seat without disruption.

⇨ To help the student with ADHD handle daily changes and problems, he needs to learn how to anticipate and handle problem situations. On a regular basis, lead the student through practice and real situations so he can acquire appropriate skills. A Problem Solving Worksheet is provided on pages 209-210 for students to learn and apply one problem-solving technique.

⇨ Don't punish or take away privileges for poor behavior or incomplete work. Students with ADHD need instruction on how to behave and how to pay better attention. They need lots of repetition and reminding. Punishing or withholding privileges is often unfair in dealing with behaviors over which they have little control.

⇨ Set aside time to teach your ADHD students social skills. Encourage them to make eye contact, to listen, and to learn conversation skills. Role-play how to enter a conversation and discuss how interrupting or changing the topic affects their peers' feelings and acceptance.

⇨ Use small group instruction as much as possible so the student with ADHD can maintain better attention. He can also fine tune appropriate social interaction and behavior skills with fewer students involved.

⇨ Avoid reacting or overreacting to the student's so-called "misbehavior." Often, the student with ADHD simply hasn't learned an appropriate behavior to replace the one he's exhibiting. Teach the student to express his needs and feelings before becoming frustrated.

⇨ If a student's inappropriate behaviors appear chronic and unchanged, observe when and where the behavior occurs most. Take steps to change any environmental causes or any needs for changes in accommodations that may improve behavior.

⇨ Some students may need more structured behavior plans to help them learn appropriate behaviors. Use My Behavior Plan on page 211 to help the student first learn to monitor and improve his own behaviors. Be sure to inform the student's parents and other teachers about the plan so they can support you and the student.

⇨ The student will need external reinforcement or consequences for his appropriate behavior when he uses a behavior plan. Let the student generate a list of incentives he'll work for. Incentives can be actual items like stickers or candy, or activities like listening to a CD or free time in the computer lab.

⇨ Be creative in determining other incentives for appropriate behavior. For example, a student who inconsistently takes his medication could earn a signed pass from the school nurse each time he does take his medication. The passes can then be converted to extra credit classroom points or to points that accumulate for a specified reward.

⇨ Enlist the support of other teachers to provide a consistent approach in managing a student's behavior. Have the student use a Weekly Classroom Progress Report like the one on page 212 in each of his classes to help monitor his progress. Behaviors could be determined based on his IEP or 504 plan or those areas showing greater need. Set up a reward system based on the number of checkmarks for the week in an individual class or for each day's classes overall, depending on where problem areas occur. Increase the checkmarks required for incentives as the student improves.

⇨ Involve and inform your school administrator, school psychologist, and guidance counselor when appropriate, especially if a behavior plan is an interim strategy to your school's discipline policy. This team, along with the parents, may need to create a stronger behavior plan as part of the student's 504 plan or IEP.

⇨ Enlist support from the student's parents as much as possible. Encourage parents to follow through with behavioral expectations and consequences at home. Share your classroom rules with them. Consistency between home and school is crucial to having a student make effective long-term growth in behavior skills. Use the Family Letter on page 212 to enlist their support.

⇨ Suggest to parents that they set up behavioral rules and expectations at home too. They're usually eager to help their child become responsible and independent both at home and at school. Provide a copy of Tips for Parents of a Child with ADHD on page 213 and the Responsible Behavior Chart on page 214 as a model for them to follow. Encourage them to share results with you from time to time.

Problem Solving Worksheet (Sample)

Every day new and different things will happen to you. Sometimes these will be problems, while other times they may be changes you need to adjust to. Use the problem-solving technique below to help you when you need to think through a situation.

Example

1. Describe the situation or problem.
   I'm late to class because I can't get my locker open.

2. List two results of the situation or problem.
   a. *I'm tardy all the time.*
   b. *I don't have the materials I need.*

3. Tell what feelings you have about the situation or problem.
   a. *I don't like teachers being angry with me.*
   b. *I wish my locker was closer to my classes.*

4. Make a list of three things you could do to solve the problem or handle the situation.
   a. *carry everything with me all day*
   b. *talk to someone in the office about getting a closer locker*
   c. *share a locker with a friend*

5. Which of the three things above do you think is best to do? Why?
   "Ask to get a closer locker" because I'd save time and not have to carry everything.

6. Try out your solution! How did it go?
   At first the office people told me "no," but then I got my guidance counselor to help me.

Now it's your turn! Use the form on the next page to solve your problem.

Problem Solving Worksheet

1. Describe the situation or problem.

   _____

   _____

   _____

2. List two results of the situation or problem.

   a. _____

   b. _____

3. Tell what feelings you have about the situation or problem.

   _____

   _____

   _____

   _____

4. Make a list of three things you could do to solve the problem or handle the situation.

   a. _____

   b. _____

   c. _____

5. Which of the three things above do you think is best to do? Why?

   _____

   _____

   _____

6. Try out your solution! How did it go?

   _____

   _____

   _____

My Behavior Plan

My Name _____   Date _____

1. I need to work on my behavior: (Put a checkmark in the appropriate boxes.)

    ❑   in the classroom
    ❑   in the lunchroom
    ❑   on the playground
    ❑   during free time

2. I'm having problems with _____

    _____

    _____

3. I think I'm having these problems because _____

    _____

    _____

4. I can improve my behavior by _____

    _____

    _____

5. The consequences of improving my behavior will be _____

    _____

    _____

    _____
               Student

    _____
               Teacher

    _____
               Parent

Weekly Classroom Progress Report

Student _____   Week of _____

Class _____   Teacher _____

	Monday	Tuesday	Wednesday	Thursday	Friday
was prepared with materials					
stayed on-task					
had good behavior					
completed assignment					

Family Letter

Dear Parent or Guardian,

Hello and welcome to the new school year! I will be working with your child this year to help him or her do well in school. I realize you have valuable insight about your child and can help me very much in being successful with him or her. It is very important that we work together to have the year go smoothly.

I've enclosed a copy of *Tips for Parents of a Child with ADHD* that I hope you will find helpful. The tips cover ways you can help your child learn and practice appropriate behaviors as well as helping him or her with schoolwork.

I will also keep you informed about your child's progress at school and enlist your help when needed.

Please feel free to call me with any concerns or questions at _____. I look forward to working with you and your child this year.

Sincerely,

_____
Resource Teacher

Tips for Parents of a Child with ADHD

Helping your child cope with his or her attention deficit hyperactivity disorder (ADHD) is an ongoing process. It requires a team effort between home and school. Support the efforts your child's teachers make to help him or her improve behavior and academic performance. Use the following tips and strategies for working with your child at home so he or she can develop the behaviors needed to do well in school and life.

1. Set up your own behavioral expectations at home. An example of a Responsible Behavior Chart is included to help coordinate efforts between home and school. The chart can be taped to the refrigerator as a way to help your child monitor progress in his or her behavior.

   The behaviors included are only a suggestion for what to include but do reflect some common areas of concern for children with ADHD. Whatever behaviors you include, choose just a few key behaviors that you feel your child can work on daily to cause significant change at home and in school.

2. Patience and understanding are key as your child works to improve behaviors and become more responsible. Calmly remind your child what he or she needs to do without nagging or shouting. Your child may need you to walk through with him or her again step-by-step how to do what's expected until he or she can remember on his or her own. When your child succeeds, praise or reward his or her efforts.

3. Let teachers know if there are any unusual circumstances that may be affecting your child's behavior in school or at home. Some students with ADHD have difficulty adjusting to change. Watch for signs from your son or daughter and share any significant ones with your child's teachers if needed.

4. Often, students may experience frustration about events at school but are hesitant or unable to express their feelings or needs to others. If your child expresses frustration about school while at home, decide if the information should be shared with his or her teachers. Most teachers appreciate such information and will help solve any problems that arise.

5. Ask for more communication from teachers if you want more information about how your child is doing. Teachers are usually quite willing to return phone calls, send home notes, or communicate through e-mail. They realize the most effective way to help students is by acting as a team with you, the parent.

6. If your school is using a behavior plan with your child, ask for a copy of the plan and any weekly progress reports related to the plan or other relevant information. Such information can help you reinforce appropriate behaviors at home and support teachers' efforts at school.

continued on next page

7. Keep the focus on the positive. You want to see your child's behavior improve and his or her social and problem-solving skills grow. Use school feedback to discuss behaviors with your child so he or she can learn from situations, but don't use it for punishment.

8. Let your child's teachers and the school nurse know if medication issues may be affecting your child's behavior. If medication has been started, changed, or stopped, your child's behavior may be inconsistent for weeks.

9. Have a special area for your child to do homework in. Use a kitchen timer to help set limits for how long your child needs to focus and work. Also have a special time each day when you talk to your child about the good things that happened in school.

Responsible Behavior Chart

Name _____   Week of _____

	Sun	Mon	Tue	Wed	Thur	Fri	Sat
Show good manners at the table							
Complete my chores							
Complete my homework							
Organize my materials for school							
Discuss tomorrow's schedule							

Rewards or Consequences _____

_____

_____

Comments _____

_____

Resources

Reading/Writing

Don Johnston, Incorporated
www.donjohnston.com
1-800-999-4660

Franklin Electronic Publishers
Reading & Writing Tools Catalog
www.franklin.com
1-800-266-5626

Georgia Department of Education
Library for the Blind
1150 Murphy Avenue, S.W.
Atlanta, GA 30310
404-756-4619

J. Weston Walch Publisher
www.walch.com
1-800-341-6094

National Library Service for the
Blind and Physically Handicapped
Library of Congress
Washington, D.C. 20542
1-800-248-6701

Recorded Books (Recording for the Blind)
20 Roszel Road
Princeton, NJ 08540
1-800-221-4792

REMEDIA Publications
www.remedia.com
1-800-826-4740

Riverdeep Interactive Learning Limited
www.riverdeep.com
1-617-995-1000

Math

Classroom Direct (distributor of technology materials)
www.classroomdirect.com
1-800-599-3040

Don Johnston, Incorporated
www.donjohnston.com
1-800-999-4660

Educational Resources
www.educationalresources.com
1-800-860-7004

GAMCO Educational Software
www.gamco.com
1-800-351-1404

J. Weston Walch Publisher
www.walch.com
1-800-341-6094

Lakeshore Learning Materials
www.lakeshorelearning.com
1-800-428-4414

PCI Educational Publishing: Special Education
www.pcicatalog.com
1-800-594-4263

PEP Registry of Educational Software Publishers
(a comprehensive listing of educational software companies with direct links to their sites)
www.microweb.com/pepsite/Software/Publishers/S.html

REMEDIA Publications
www.remedia.com
1-800-826-4740

Riverdeep Interactive Learning Limited
www.riverdeep.com
1-617-995-1000

References

CHADD (Children and Adults with Attention-Deficit/Hyperactivity Disorder). Fact Sheet #1: *The Disorder Named AD/HD.* www.chadd.org

Conti-D'Antonio, Marcia, et. al. *Supporting Students with Learning Needs in the Block.* Larchmont, NY: Eye on Education, Inc., 1998.

Diagnostic and Statistical Manual of the American Psychiatric Association, 4th Edition (DSM-IV, 1994).

Dornbush, Marilyn P., Ph.D and Pruitt, Sheryl K., M. Ed. *Teaching the Tiger: A Handbook for Individuals Involved in the Education of Students with Attention Deficit Disorders, Tourette Syndrome or Obsessive-Compulsive Disorder.* Duarte, CA: Hope Press, 1997.

Flick, Grad L., Ph. D. *ADD/ADHD Behavior-Change Resource Kit:Ready-to-Use Strategies & Activities for Helping Children with Attention Deficit Disorder.* NY: The Center for Applied Research in Education, 1998.

Friend, Marilyn and Bursuck, William D. *Including Students with Special Needs: A Practical Guide for Classroom Teachers.* Needham Heights, MA: Allyn & Bacon, 1999.

Greenberg, Gregory S. and Horn, Wade F. *Attention Deficit Hyperactivity Disorder: Questions and Answers for Parents.* Champaign, IL: Research Press, 1991.

Hallowell, Edward M., M.D. and Ratey, John J., M.D. *Driven to Distraction: Recognizing and Coping with Attention Deficit Disorder from Childhood Through Adulthood.* NY: Pantheon Books, 1994.

Hammeken, Peggy A. *Inclusion: 450 Strategies for Success, A Practical Guide for All Educators Who Teach Students with Disabilities.* Minnetonka, MN: Peytral Publications, 1997.

Khalsa, SiriNam S. *The Inclusive Classroom: A Practical Guide for Educators.* Glenview, IL: Good Year Books, 1999.

Markel, Geraldine and Greenbaum, Judith. *Performance Breakthroughs for Adolescents with Learning Disabilities or ADD: How to Help Students Succeed in the Regular Education Classroom.* Champaign, IL: Research Press, 1996.

Sears, William, M.D. and Thompson, Lynda, Ph. D. *The A.D.D. Book: Understandings, New Approaches to Parenting Your Child.* NY: Little, Brown and Company, 1998.

Warren, Paul, M.D. and Capehart, Jody, M. Ed. with Sandy Dengler. *You & Your A.D.D. Child: How to Understand and Help Kids with Attention Deficit Disorder.* Nashville, TN: Thomas Nelson Publishers, Inc., 1995.

19-02-987654321